WEST CORNWALL MINERAL RALWAYS

Maurice Dart

Cover picture: Locomotives of class 66 now work all traffic over the surviving lines, which serve the china clay industry in mid Cornwall. No.66220 stands on the running line at Central Treviscoe whilst shunting empty CDA wagons into Kernick siding on 1st August 2000. (M.Dart)

Published February 2005

ISBN 1 904474 48 9

© Middleton Press, 2005

Design Deborah Esher

Published by
    Middleton Press
    Easebourne Lane
    Midhurst, West Sussex
    GU29 9AZ
Tel: 01730 813169
Fax: 01730 812601
Email: info@middletonpress.co.uk
www.middletonpress.co.uk

Printed & bound by Biddles Ltd, Kings Lynn

CONTENTS

1	Treffrys Tramway-Hendra Crazey to Newquay Harbour	1-10
2	Treamble Branch	11-15
3	Lansalson Branch	16-23
4	Trenance Sidings	24
5	Burngullow	25-30
6	Cornwall Junction Branch-Burngullow to St.Dennis Junction	31-67
7	Retew Branch-St.Dennis Junction to Meledor Mill	68-85
8	Newham Branch	86-88
9	Falmouth Docks Branch	89-94
10	Tresevean Branch	95-100
11	Portreath Branch	101-108
12	North Crofty Branch	109-110
13	Roskear Branch	111-112
14	Hayle Wharves Branch	113-118
15	Albert Quay Siding, Penzance	119-120

ACKNOWLEDGMENTS

I express my thanks to the photographers who have provided copies of their own photographs and to those who have agreed for me to use material from their collections. They are named in the credits. I thank the Cornwall Railway Society and the Branch Line Society for permission to use their material. I also thank Mrs R.Barrett, I. Bowditch, P.Bragg, P.Butt, A.R.Cooke, B.Gibson, Mrs J.Green, S.Hegginbotham, K.Jenkin, S.Jenkins, N.Langridge and Mrs G.Searle for their help. I am most grateful for the patience and assistance of the staff of the Cornwall Studies Library at Redruth.

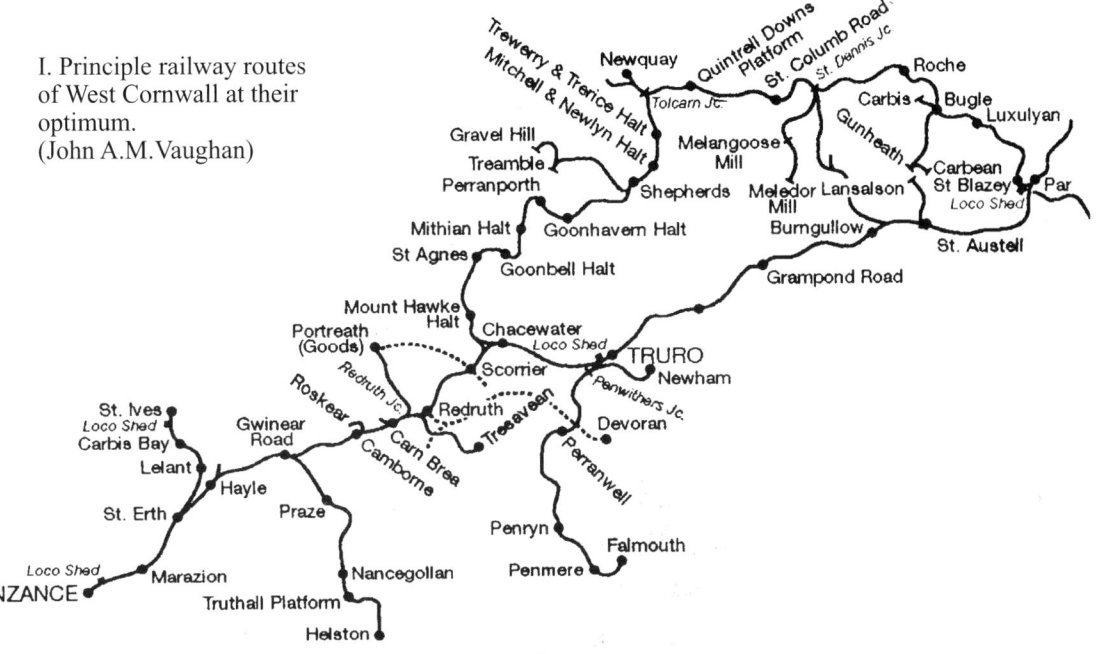

I. Principle railway routes of West Cornwall at their optimum. (John A.M.Vaughan)

INDEX

Blackpool	29
Bojea	19
Boskell	22
Burngullow	25, 31
Burngullow West	32
Burgotha	80
Calenick Bridge	86
Carlyon Farm	16
Carn Brea	108
Carpella	34
Carloggos	41
Central Treviscoe	56
Cornish Kaolin	27
Crugwallins	33
Domellick	62
Drinnick Mill	36, 47
Drinnick Low Level Lines	41
Fairfield Crossing	103
Falmouth Docks	89
Goonvean	49
Great Treviscoe	54
Grove	75
Gulleys Wharf	2
Hayle	113
Hayle Wharves	115
Hendra Crazey	1
Illogan Highway	102
Kernick	54
Lanner Hill	98
Lansalson	23
Little Treviscoe	52
Lower Ruddle	21
Melangoose Mill	74
Melbur	81
Meledor Mill	82
Methrose	28
Nanpean Wharf	39
New Halwyn	73
Newham	87
New Meledor	85
Newquay Harbour	7
New Trerice	69
North Crofty	109
Parkandillack	58
Penzance, Albert Quay	119
Pochins Wharf	63
Portreath Harbour	106
Portreath Incline	104
Portreath Junction	101
Retew	70
Roskear	111
Ruthvoes	4
Shepherds	11
South Fraddon	72
St Dennis Junction	64
Tolbenny	79
Toldish Tunnel	5
Treamble	12
Trelavour	60
Trenance Sidings	24
Trerice	69
Tresevean Incline	95
Tresevean Mine	100
Trethosa	53
Trethowel	20
Virginia	77
West of England Company Siding	48
West Treviscoe	78
Wheal Beauchamp	98
Wheal Benallick	74
Wheal Louisa	26
Whitegates (St Dennis)	62

GEOGRAPHICAL SETTING

The area covered by this book lies west of the St.Austell River and the River Camel. Included is the large central granite mass of Hensbarrow Downs, which continues west, and forms the backbone of the county. This is surrounded by Old Red Sandstone, which is penetrated by the River Fal, the Red River and other shorter rivers. The granite at Hensbarrow has undergone transformation to china clay, which is otherwise known as kaolin. Further to the west it contains numerous metallic deposits. The metal extraction and the china clay industries required transport for their products to reach the coast, so a network of lines evolved to meet those requirements. The lines which served the china clay industry were severely graded and possessed three tunnels, one of which is still used by passenger trains. There were also two cable worked inclines. Further west, as the county narrowed, the lines were shorter and with gentler gradients. However, there were two cable worked inclines in this area. The maps are to the scale of 6 ins. to 1 mile unless otherwise stated.

HISTORICAL BACKGROUND

Copper, tin, arsenic and other metals have been mined in West Cornwall from at least the mid seventeenth century. As the engineering industry developed, improved methods of mining were introduced which increased the output from the mines. Ore had been carried to the smelting works and harbours, and supplies taken back, by pack horses and wagons. These travelled over rough hilly tracks that became deeply rutted. To facilitate transport light tramways were laid to connect the mines to the smelters and harbours. Sailing and steamships carried the products to their destinations. The china clay industry also developed in the nineteenth century and a system of light tramways evolved to transport the material to harbours. With the arrival of the main line railway companies, standard gauge lines replaced some of the tramways. The first standard gauge line to arrive was the Hayle Railway, which opened its first lines in 1837. It later became the property of the West Cornwall Railway, which eventually became part of the GWR. The GWR became the Western Region of British Railways on nationalisation on 1st January 1948. Further historical details may be found at the commencement of each section.

1. TREFFRYS TRAMWAY-HENDRA CRAZEY to NEWQUAY HARBOUR

This line was built to serve china clay works on Hendra Downs above St.Dennis. It was a horse worked tramway, which opened in sections, from Newquay, from 1846, and the final section to Newquay Harbour was opened in November 1849. The Cornwall Minerals Railway was incorporated on 21st July 1873, purchased the Treffrys tramways and improved it, with diversions, to carry locomotive worked traffic. The old route closed and the new route opened on 1st June 1874. A further re-alignment east of Tolcarn junction was opened on 8th May 1904. The incline from Hendra Crazey was closed, but a short section approaching Whitegates siding, at St.Dennis, was retained until 1914. The line from Newquay to the harbour closed during 1926. Parkandillack to St.Dennis junction yard closed on 6th February 1966.

HENDRA CRAZEY

1. The top of the incline has long disappeared into Hendra clay pit. To reach the pit the line burrowed beneath a road. Here, we look north west from the road on 17th April 1991. The trackbed descended as a defile towards the lower road, on which the buildings stand. It tunnelled beneath the lower road. The lower portal of the tunnel is open and could be accessed by climbing into, and along, a deep cutting. This appears on map XIV. (M.Dart)

2. To the right of the friendly horse we see a bank and bushes. This was Gulleys Wharf, on the lower part of the Hendra incline. It is seen looking south on 10th June 1989. Steps which led to the wharf now form part of a footpath. (M.Dart)

3. Two trackbeds are featured in this view, that looks east on 17th June 1989. The ancient bridge passed beneath the bottom section of the Hendra incline. The gate is open across the new line from Parkandillack to St.Dennis junction. The two routes converged and joined at Whitegates, St.Dennis. (M.Dart)

RUTHVOES/TOLDISH

II. The CMR route through Toldish tunnel is shown on this 1908 map, with an occupation bridge to the east. The original route at the west end of the deviation is shown. This was replaced by the present alignment on 15th May 1904.

4. St. Dennis Junction was formerly called Bodmin Road Junction and St.Columb Road was formerly called Halloon. The tramway followed a direct route between them, which ran in a deep cutting and through a tunnel, which could not be widened to accommodate steam traction. We look almost east, during a visit by members of the Branch Line Society on 1st June 1994, to a bridge, which crossed the cutting at Ruthvoes. (M.Dart)

TOLDISH TUNNEL

5. This part of the route contained the 530yd Toldish, or Ruthvoes (pronounced locally as Ruthers) Tunnel which was too restricted to accommodate locomotives. This extremely unusual view from inside the eastern portal of the tunnel was taken during the BLS visit on 1st June 1994. The ground had been built up, to a few steps behind the photographer, to contain water that had flooded the tunnel for half its length. The narrowness of the bore is apparent. The vegetation-choked cutting is beyond. (M.Dart)

6. We look at the west portal of the tunnel on 10th July 1966. Inside was a reservoir which formed part of the water supply to Newquay. A roof collapse at the mid-point has blocked the bore. This doorway was securely sealed by May 2000. The portal was guarded by a dense mass of brambles. (M.Dart)

NEWQUAY HARBOUR

III. The passenger terminus features in the centre of this 1907 map. The line to the harbour curves west and then north to pass through the tunnel.

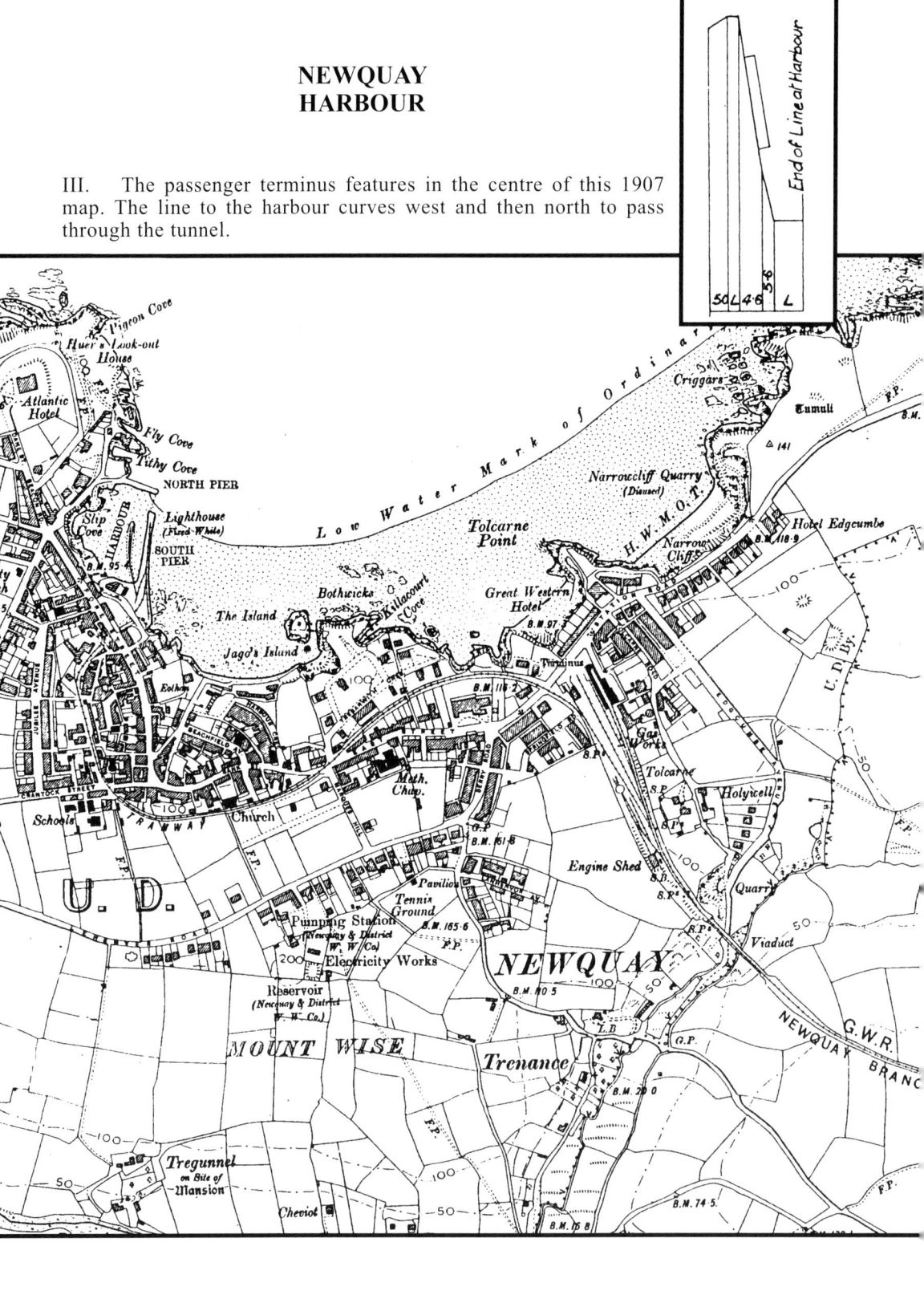

7. The line followed a curving course from the station. This is now a footpath, known as the Tramlines. The route was spanned by a bridge which is viewed looking west on 7th November 1987. (M.Dart)

8. The line descended on gradients of 1 in 4.6 and 5.6, in a 80yd tunnel, to reach the harbour. The upper portal was sealed when the line closed. During construction work at the end of October 1987, the long forgotten portal was unexpectedly unearthed. It is viewed, looking north, on 2nd November. The portal is beneath the floor of a warehouse, but a trap door and steps have been provided to permit access for maintenance. (B.S.J.White Press Photography)

9. We look south east from the harbour on 28th May 1922, and see the lower portal of the tunnel which was bricked up after closure. During the 1960s an aquarium was established in the lower portion of the tunnel. A wall was constructed to seal it from the upper section but a door provided access for maintenance purposes. The aquarium moved to another location in the late 1990s, since when this portal has been closed. (M.Dart coll.)

10. A panorama of the harbour in the early 1900s shows sidings which served the quays; they converged at the lower left towards the tunnel. The central quay is now severed from the land. (M.Dart coll.)

Further photographs appear in *Branch Lines to Newquay.*

2. TREAMBLE BRANCH

This line served iron mines in the Perran lode which was southwest of Newquay and northeast of Perranporth. Following the demise of the mines the line was closed. After a period of closure it was reopened to goods, as quarries had opened and a gunpowder factory had been started in the area. During the Second World War the line saw a few trains carrying military personnel to camps which had been established on Penhale Downs. Treffrys Tramway had opened a line from Treloggan (later renamed Tolcarne) Junction to East Wheal Rose on 26th February 1849. The CMR opened a route from East Wheal Rose to Treamble on 1st June 1874. A further line that ran from Treamble to Gravel Hill mine opened on the same date. This section was built without the landowner's consent, closed during 1888, the track being removed in November 1889. From Deer Park siding, a narrow gauge tramway, which closed in 1886, led to the like named mine. Shepherds to Treamble closed on 1st January 1917 and the track was lifted. Track was relaid during December 1925 and the line was re-opened in February 1926; it closed finally on 1st January 1952.

June 1879

TREAMBLE AND GRAVEL HILL BRANCHES.

DOWN TRAINS.					UP TRAINS.				
Distances from Newquay	STATIONS.	GOODS and Minerals. 1 arr pass dep			Distances from Gravel Hill.	STATIONS.	GOODS and Minerals. 1 arr pass dep		
		p.m. R. R.					p.m. R. R.		
—	Newquay	2 0 s. s.	…	…	—	Gravel Hill	…	…	…
¾	Tolcarn Junction	2 3 2 4	…	…	1	Treamble	2 45	…	…
1¼	Trevemper Siding	C. R.	…	…	3	Deer Park Siding	C. R.	…	…
4½	East Wheal Rose Sg	C. R.	…	…	4¾	Shepherd Siding	C. R.	…	…
6	Shepherd Siding	C. R.	…	…	5¾	East Wheal Rose Sg	C. R.	…	…
7½	Deer Park Siding	C. R.	…	…	9	Trevemper Siding	C. R.	…	…
9¼	Treamble	2 40	…	…	9½	Tolcarn Junction	3 25 3 26 s. s.	…	…
10¼	Gravel Hill		…	…	10¼	Newquay	3 30	…	…

SHEPHERDS AND TREAMBLE.

Single Line, worked by Wooden Train Staff. One engine in steam. Freight Trains only. Speed not to exceed 15 miles per hour.

Down Trains.			Week Days only.			Up Trains.	
M.	C.	STATIONS.	Ruling Gradient 1 in	Freight. RR ¶ MWF		STATIONS.	Freight. RR ¶ MWF
				a.m.	a.m.		a.m.
—	—	SHEPHERDS	—	—	11 30	TREAMBLE	11 55
—	49	Stop Board	—	1139 P	11 40	Treamble Loop	—
2	59	Stop Board	—	1141 P	11 43	SHEPHERDS	12 10
3	2	Treamble Loop	40 F	—	—		
3	14	TREAMBLE	—	11 45	—		

¶—Suspended.

1951

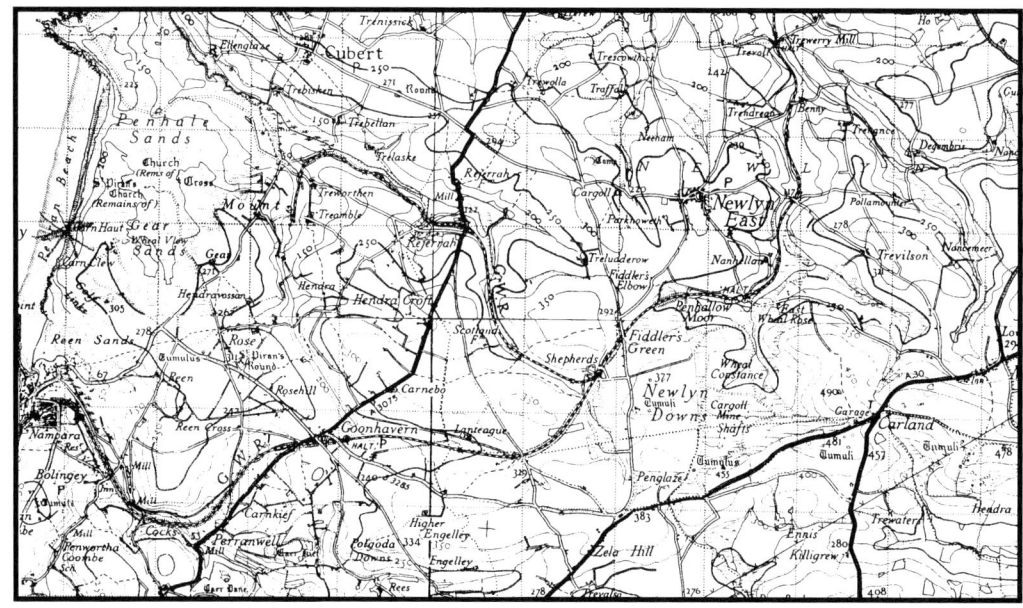

IV. The 1930 map at 1ins to 1 mile shows the Perranporth to Newquay line and the junction at Shepherds. The branch to Treamble curves north-west to Rejerrah, where an overline bridge still exists. At Treworthen the branch turned south to Treamble.

SHEPHERDS

11. Looking south in August 1948, we see the branch to Treamble as it diverged from the Newquay to Perranporth line. After closure, a short stub was retained for PW Dept use. (P.J.Garland/R.S.Carpenter)

TREAMBLE

12. We look north in the 1930s and see 0-6-0PT no.1794. It is about to pass through a gate, which marked the limit of GWR ownership, to enter the terminus. (C.Benney coll.)

V. This 1908 map at 6ins to 1 mile includes the terminus and part of the trackbed of the old line to Gravel Hill Mine. Narrow gauge tramways were once located on the east side of the terminus at Treamble.

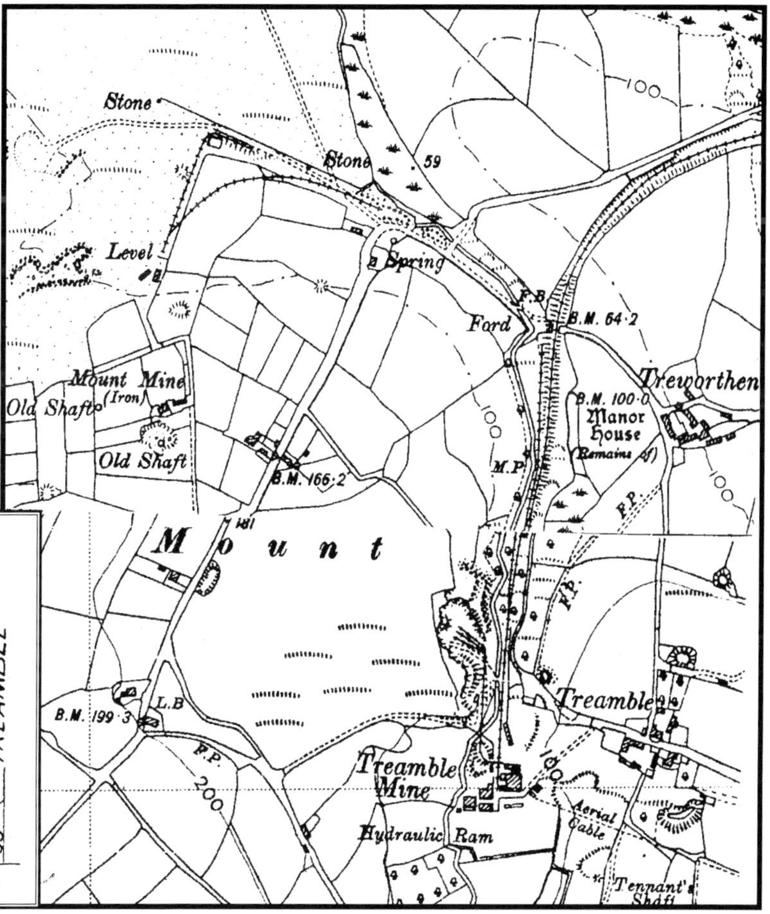

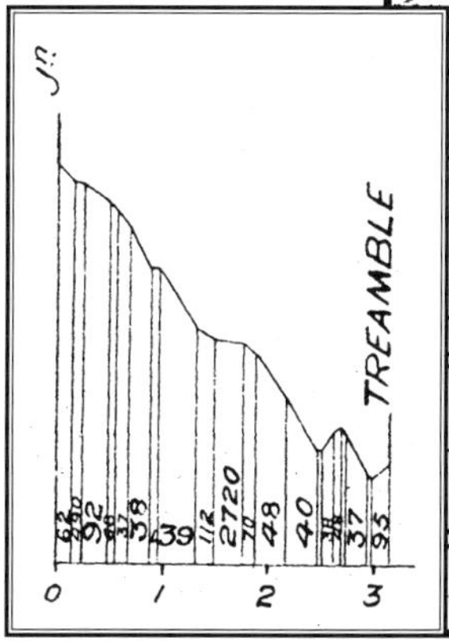

13. This view looks south west at the terminus in the 1930s where shunting is in progress. The structure that crossed the line carried a narrow gauge tramway that connected quarries to the mills of the C.M.Powder Co.Ltd.
(C.Benney coll.)

14. We look north in the 1930s and see wagons alongside the loading wharf, and various buildings, which appear somewhat derelict.
(C.Benney coll.)

Further scenes are included in *Branch Lines to Newquay*.

15. This rare view of a train at the terminus which was taken in the 1930s, includes 0-6-0PT no.1794. We look north east towards the 2ft gauge tramway which passed above the line.
(C.Benney coll.)

3. LANSALSON BRANCH

VI. A map from 1938 shows the entire line. Carlyon Farm kilns are on the right, near Trethowel, just north of which is Bojea yard. Lower Ruddle wharf is on the right, after the bridge over the main road. Boskell sidings are on the left. Lansalson Wharf is at Ruddlemoor. Trenance sidings are on the north side of the main line, west of Trenance Junction.

This line was a latecomer, built to serve the china clay industry in the Trenance Valley. An extension of the Pentewan Railway had been proposed on this route but was not built. On 26th July 1910, the GWR was authorised to construct the line but the World War One delayed this. The section to Bojea sidings opened on 1st May 1920, and the extension to Lansalson followed a few weeks later, on 24th May. Closure beyond Lower Lansalson took place on 27th July 1964. The remainder closed on 6th May 1968.

OPENING AND CLOSING DATES OF SIDINGS

	Opened	Closed
Carlyon Farm	1929/30	27th July 1964
Bojea	1st May 1920	August 1964
Lower Ruddle	NA	6th May 1968
Boskell	NA	6th May 1968
Lansalson	24th May 1920	30th October 1962

September 1924

TRENANCE VALLEY BRANCH.
GOODS TRAINS ONLY.

Single Line. Worked by Wooden Train Staff, lettered Trenance Junction and Lansalson.
Speed of all Trains not to exceed 10 miles per hour.

[Down and Up trains timetable with stations: Trenance Junction, Loverings Siding, Bojea Sidings, Lower Ruddle and Boskell Sidings, Lansalson]

ST. AUSTELL, TRENANCE JUNCTION AND LANSALSON.
Freight Trains only.

SINGLE LINE WORKED BY TRAIN STAFF.
THE SPEED OF TRAINS ON THIS BRANCH MUST NOT EXCEED 10 MILES AN HOUR.

[Down and Up trains timetable, 1951]

VII. A survey from 1938 shows the double line branch leaving Trenance Junction. It became single line before it passed over the occupation crossing at Menacuddle.

1951

CARLYON FARM

16. From Trenance Junction the line was double for a short distance. Soon after the line became single, it passed over Menacuddle occupation crossing. Carlyon Farm siding was on the down side, a further 300yd along the line. All ground frames that controlled sidings on the china clay branch lines possessed name boards. On 24th November 1956 the author is seen gripping the point lever at the mispelt, Carlyon Farm Siding South ground frame. (M.Daly)

17. This scene looks south from Bojea yard to Carlyon Farm siding and kiln on 19th May 1968. Several of the wagons that ran on the narrow gauge tramways are visible. Fellow author Michael Messenger is examining some of them. (M.Dart)

18. We look east in the early 1930s across the Trenance Valley to Carlyon Farm kiln which has the press house and furnace in the centre. Wagons are on the siding alongside the loading area to which clay was carried from within by two narrow gauge tramways. The gradient of 1 in 40 is very noticeable. (Imerys Minerals)

BOJEA

19. Looking northward, 0-6-0PT no.3705 is alongside Carlyon Farm siding on 13th September 1956. The first terminus of the branch, at Bojea sidings, is in the distance. The line to Lansalson is on the extreme right. (H.Davies)

TRETHOWEL

20. The line climbed at 1 in 40 from Bojea sidings to cross the Bodmin Road at Trethowel. A Western National bus is heading for St.Austell, as we look north, on 11th May 1968. This view was taken from a special train organised by Plymouth Railway Circle. The stacks of several clay kilns are visible. (M.Dart)

LOWER RUDDLE

21. We follow the line across the main road from St.Austell to Bodmin, and look north, in June 1958 to see no.4552 at Lower Ruddle sidings. The running line can be seen just above the engine's front buffer. To the left of its cab wagons stand in Boskell sidings, which were on a higher level. (N.Simmons/H.Davies photos.)

BOSKELL

22. Boskell sidings trailed in on the down side a short distance farther along the branch. We look south west in June 1958, as 2-6-2T no.4552 shunts a long rake of wagons. These sidings crossed a substantial bridge over the St.Austell River. (N.Simmons/H.Davies photos.)

LANSALSON

23. A special train, formed of eleven brake vans, ran on 28th April 1962 for Plymouth Railway Circle. We look south east to see it leaving Lansalson yard, headed by 2-6-2Ts 4564 and 5518, to return along the line. Also shown is part of Ruddlemoor village, chimney stacks of the derelict Ruddle kilns and overgrown settling tanks of Lansalson china clay works. (M.Dart coll.)

4. TRENANCE SIDINGS.

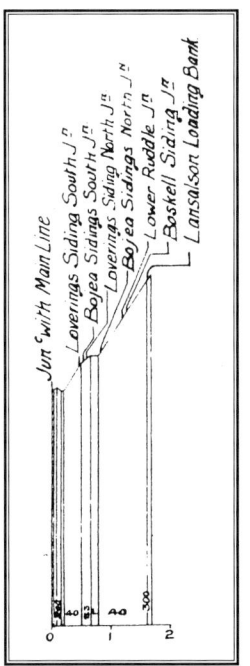

These were on the up side of the main line, slightly less than one mile west of St.Austell; they served Carroncarrow and Trenance china clay kilns. Originally there was one siding which was extended to connect into the main line at its west end, to form a loop, in November 1893. Further developments, which included the addition of a second loop, took place in 1899. Following cessation of drying at the kilns, the sidings closed on 25th September 1966; they were on a separate formation that was remote from the running line. A steep road, which passed beneath the main line, required a separate bridge under the sidings. The two kilns were on opposite sides of the road and were level with the railway.

Further photographs appear in the *St.Austell to Penzance* album.

24. We look north east at the sidings in the 1920s. Wagons are alongside Carroncarrow kiln. A loop line passed in front of Trenance sidings signal box and Trenance kiln, and the twin bridges over the road to Greensplat, are to the right, but out of view. (Imerys Minerals)

5. BURNGULLOW

These sidings were on the up side of the main line, east of the site of the first station at Burngullow; they served china clay kilns and a loading wharf. Wheal Louisa siding was at the east end and Cornish Kaolin (Tehidy Minerals) was at the west end. When Burngullow kilns were built, lines were laid which connected the sidings. Parkyn & Peters (Tehidy Minerals) later opened a siding, a little to the east. This was extended across a bridge over a minor road to Methrose siding. The layout was modified over the years to serve additional kilns. This was completely remodelled early in 1989 to serve a new china clay slurry plant, from where the "Silver Bullet" train operated to the Caledonian Paper Mills at Irvine. The pan kilns had closed but their linhays were utilised for storing clay dried elsewhere, and sidings remained to serve them. Some of the older sidings remained in place but were disconnected at one or both ends. The location was called Burngullow until the slurry plant was built, since when it has been called Blackpool, which is the name of of the massive clay pit to its north. China clay drying and slurry production ceased here in September 2003.

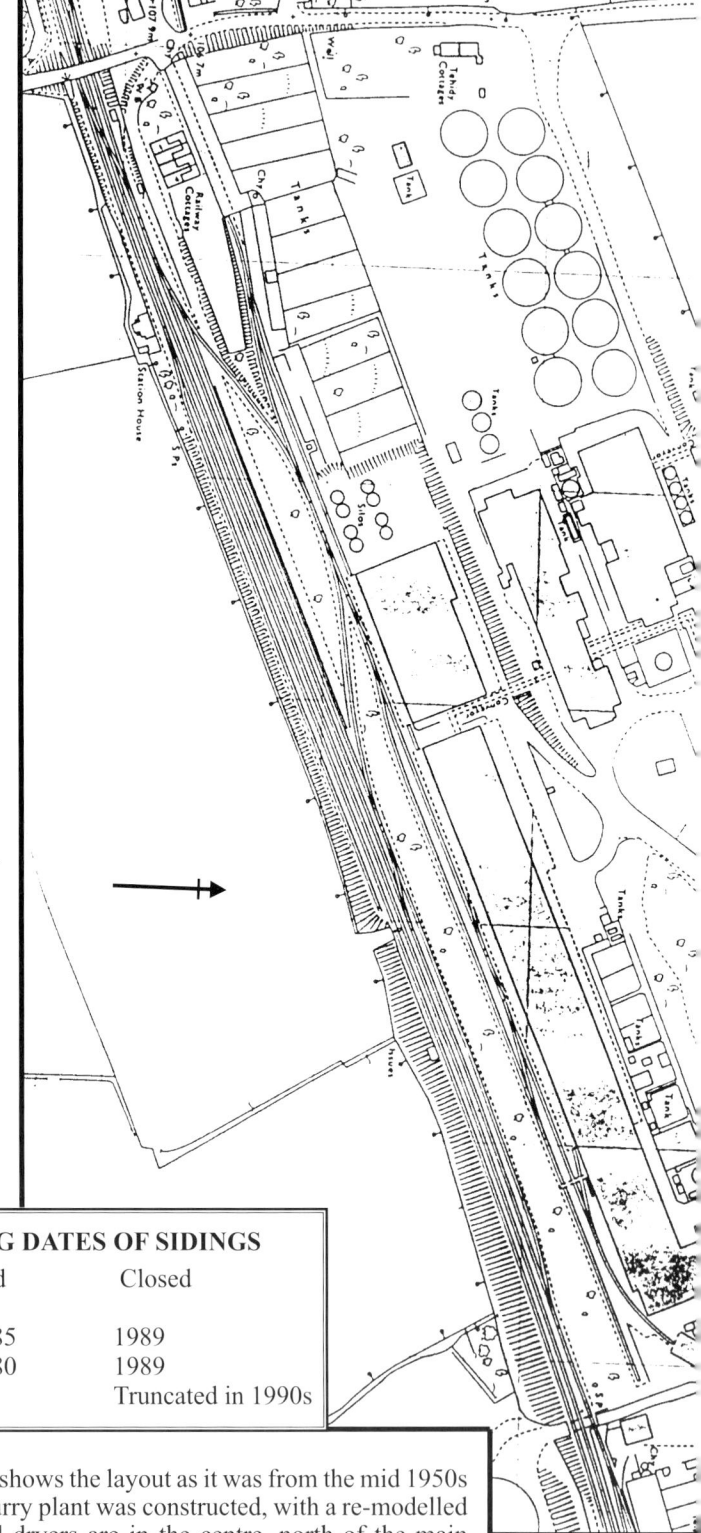

OPENING AND CLOSING DATES OF SIDINGS

	Opened	Closed
Methrose	30th July 1923	
Parkyn & Peters	15th August 1885	1989
Wheal Louisa	30th August 1880	1989
Cornish Kaolin	15th June 1885	Truncated in 1990s

VIII. This 20 inch to the mile map shows the layout as it was from the mid 1950s to the early 1989, before the new slurry plant was constructed, with a re-modelled track layout. Burngullow kilns and dryers are in the centre, north of the main lines. The Wheal Louisa line curves off at the east end as does the Cornish Kaolin route at the west end. Methrose siding is at the bottom of the map. The first station at Burngullow was by Railway Cottages. (Imerys Minerals)

BURNGULLOW

25. Since the 1880s china clay kilns here have been served by sidings on the up side of the main line. They are near to the site of the original station. In the early 1920s we look north west towards Burngullow kilns with wagons on the inside line awaiting loading from the linhays. Slightly raised ground to the left of the sidings formed a loading wharf for the transfer of clay from horse drawn wagons. Coal, which had been delivered by train, would be carried to distant kilns. (Imerys Minerals)

WHEAL LOUISA

26. Wheal Louisa siding was at the southeast end of Burngullow kilns; it curved off and ran between two banks which are seen as we look north on 3rd March 1989. A loading wharf, used by horse-drawn wagons, was situated at the top of the bank on the right. After it had been disconnected, the siding had become choked with brambles. (M.Dart)

CORNISH KAOLIN

27. Cornish Kaolin siding was opened from the west end of Burngullow kilns by Tehidy Minerals. We look west on 6th March 1989 to the siding that ran in a restricted clearance tunnel below the linhay of the kiln. Clay was loaded through hatches in the floor that were fitted with chutes. The siding, which was used as a shunting neck, contained modern tank wagons for clay slurry. It was truncated in the early 1990s by building an earth bank across the entrance to the tunnelled section. (M.Dart)

METHROSE

28. Tehidy Minerals opened Parkyn & Peters siding between the kilns and the main line. It was south of the loading bank seen in picture no 25. The Great Halviggan China Clay Co. extended it east across a bridge to form Methrose siding. We look east on 25th March 1991 when it was being utilised for storing small clay slurry tank wagons. Amey Railways established a depot on the site of the kiln in 2004 and have relaid the siding as a single line. (M.Dart)

BLACKPOOL

29. A new plant for producing high density clay slurry was constructed at Blackpool early in 1989. It was adjacent to Burngullow and the layout was modified to cater for this. This was served by connections off the branch to Drinnick Mill which, since 4th October 1986, left the now singled main line at Burngullow East, opposite Methrose siding. No. 08320 0-6-0D *Susan* was obtained from BR to work at Blackpool, but it had failed on 22nd November 1993. Looking west we see tank wagons being shunted through the plant which cleaned their interiors. The locomotive, 0-4-0DH *Denise* was on loan from Crugwallins. Disused kilns at Burngullow are on the right, whilst on the skyline are derelict silos which handled spray dried clay. The main line to Truro is far left. (M.Dart)

30. This eastward panorama from the centre of the sidings is dated 24th April 2002. Burngullow kilns are upper left. The sidings contain wagons for clay slurry and dried clay. A wagon repair facility was established in about 2001 towards the east end, where four slurry tank wasgons await attention. The stack of Methrose kiln is visible in the right background. (M.Dart)

CORNWALL JUNCTION BRANCH.

	DOWN TRAINS.				UP TRAINS.		
Distances from Drinnick Mill	STATIONS.	GOODS and Minerals.		Distances from St. Dennis Junction	STATIONS.	GOODS and Minerals.	
		arr	dep			arr	dep
		a.m.					a.m.
—	Drinnick Mill		10 30	—	St. Dennis Junction		9 20
½	W'st of Eng Co's Sg	c. a.		1¼	Whitegate Siding	c. n.	
¾	Luke's Siding	c. a.		1½	Gulley's	c. n.	
1¼	Goonvean (Slip)	c. n.		2	Parkandillack Sg	c. n.	
1½	Little Treviscoe Sg	c. a.		3	Great Treviscoe	c. n.	
1¾	Trethosa	c. n		3¼	Trethosa	c. n.	
1⅞	Great Treviscoe	c. n.		3½	Little Treviscoe	c. n.	
2¼	Parkandillack	c. n.		3¾	Goonvean (Slip)	c. n.	
3	Gulley's	c. n.		4	Luke's Siding	c. n.	
3¼	Whitegate	c. n.		4¼	W'st of Eng Co's Sg	c. n.	
4¼	St. Dennis Junction	11 45		4½	Drinnick Mill	10 20	

This Branch will be worked by the Engine leaving Par at 6·15 a.m. after returning from Newquay.

June 1879

6. CORNWALL JUNCTION BRANCH-BURNGULLOW TO ST. DENNIS JUNCTION

This route served china clay and brick works. It has also carried coal and calcified seaweed. Drinnick Mill, which was also known as Nanpean Wharf, was a public goods station. Burngullow to Drinnick Mill was authorised by the Newquay & Cornwall Junction Railway Act dated 14th July 1864 and opened on 1st July 1869. William West & Sons, contractors from St.Blazey, worked the line. On 21st July 1873 an Act transferred ownership to the CMR, who worked the line from 2nd June 1874. A dispute arose between the GWR and the Carpella United China Clay Co. over mineral rights. The question was whether china clay was a mineral and the House of Lords ruled in favour of the clay company. So a section of the line between High Street and Old Carpella was closed on 16th December 1909 to permit china clay to be worked under the formation. A line on a new formation to connect up the "Carpella Gap", was opened on 18th April 1922. It crossed the old trackbed south of Carpella and skirted the east side of Carpella Pit, to reach Old Carpella. The line terminated at a location later known as Nanpean Wharf. Sidings, which were accessed via a head-shunt, descended for several hundred yards to serve clay works at North Carloggos.

From Drinnick Mill a new line was built which served more china clay and china stone works and it provided an alternative route to Fowey other than via Burngullow. This line was built under the CMR Act dated 21st July 1873. It commenced as a new route from a junction with the line to Nanpean Wharf near Drinnick Mill. At Whitegates, it met the formation of Treffrys Tramway from Hendra Crazey, which it used to reach St.Dennis Junction. Opened on 1st June 1874, the section from Parkandillack to St.Dennis Junction yard was closed on 6th February 1966. The yard was disconnected from the line to Newquay in February 1992 and the track was lifted during October 1999.

OPENING AND CLOSING DATES OF SIDINGS

	Opened	Closed
Burngullow West	13th June 1898	September 1974
Crugwallins	23rd March 1907	
Beacon	7th March 1928	June 1963
High Street	NA	1967
New Carpella	10th August 1917	1960s
Carpella	10th March 1898	1968
Dubbers no.2	19th September 1865	4th November 1973
Dubbers no.1	19th September 1865	1974
Carloggos	19th September 1865	13th January 1993
West of England co.	19th September 1865	28th December 1975
Lukes Old	3rd March 1873	21st August 1960
Lukes New	NA	June 1963
Slip	NA	11th June 1965
Restowrack	31st December 1923	1980s
Varcoes	NA	4th January 1976
Goonvean	10th February 1882	4th January 1976
Little Treviscoe	1st March 1907	August 1969
Trethosa	NA	early 1948
Kernick	26th October 1911	
Great Treviscoe	1st July 1890	31st December 1967
Treviscoe	8th November 1911	
Central Treviscoe	12th June 1896	March 1934
	September 1965	
Parkandillack	20th May 1913	
Trelavour	NA	
Whitegates	NA	4th January 1965
Pochins	1884	1933

elangoose Mill	1903	1913	1923	1932
neral goods forwarded (tons)	14	166	52	59
al and coke received (tons)	8660	13309	10032	7743
her minerals received (tons)	240	919	1079	239
neral goods received (tons)	1051	903	657	263
ıcks of livestock handled	-	-	-	-

not available.)

Drinnick Mill	1903	1913	1923	1932	1938
General goods forwarded (tons)	3	139	270	1089	1194
Coal and coke received (tons)	27182	32830	13944	11638	15125
Other minerals received (tons)	1198	1398	748	820	632
General goods received (tons)	1990	3457	2832	1133	4042
Trucks of livestock handled	-	-	-	-	18

(* not available.)

CORNWALL JUNCTION BRANCH

Single Line. It is worked by the Electric Train Staff between St. Dennis Junction Ground Frame and Kernick, Kernick and Drinnick Mill and Drinnick Mill and Burngullow West. Crossing places, Kernick and Drinnick Mill. Goods Trains only worked on this Branch.

DOWN TRAINS. WEEK DAYS ONLY.

Distance from Burngullow M	C	STATIONS.	Station No.	Ruling Gradient 1 in	Time allowances for Ordinary Freight Trains (see page 2). Point to point times.	Allow for stop.	Allow for start.	1 K Mineral. RR	2 K Mineral.	3 K Mineral. RR	4 K Mineral. RR	5 K Mineral. RR	6 K Mineral. RR	7
					Mins.	Mins.	Mins.	A.M.	A.M.	A.M.	P.M.	P.M.	P.M.	
—	—	**Burngullow** dep.	2058	...	—	—	1	7 40	11 10	....	....	2 5	....	....
—	4	Burngullow West Sdg.	2060	50 R	—	—	—	—	—	..	..	—	..	..
—	17	Crugwallins Siding	2216	50 R	1	1	1	—	CR	....	....	CR	....	....
—	58	Langeth Crossing ..	2217	50 R	—	—	—	—	—	..	..	—	..	..
1	24	High Street Siding	2218	50 R	8	1	1	—	—	....	....	CR	....	....
2	12	Carpella Sidings ..	2219	28 R	5	1	1	—	11 25	..	..	CR	..	..
2	53	Dubbers No. 1 Siding	2220	50 R	—	—	—	—		....	....	—	....	....
2	55	Wharf Line Siding	2221	80 F	—	—	—	8 10	..	..	..	—	..	..
2	60	Drinnick Mill ..	2222	80 F	3	1	1		....	11 0	2 0	2 45	5 0	....
2	71	West of Eng. Co.'s Sdgs	2223	11 R	—	—	—	..	..	CR	CR		CR	..
3	7	Luke's Old Siding ..	2224	11 R	—	—	—	....	....	CR	CR	....	CR	....
3	26	Stop Board	—	11 R	3	1	1	..	..	P	P	..	P	..
3	22	Luke's New Siding ..	2225	40 F	—	—	—	....	....	CR	CR	....	CR	....
3	30	Stop Board	—	40 F	—	—	—	..	..	P	P	..	P	..
3	35	Slip Siding	2226	40 F	—	—	—	....	....	CR	CR	....	CR	....
3	45	Varcoe's & Goonv'nSdgs	2227	40 F	1	1	1	..	..	CR	CR	..	CR	..
3	54	Little Treviscoe Siding	2228	L.	—	—	—	....	....	CR	CR	....	CR	....
3	66	Trethosa Siding ..	2229	L.	2	1	1	..	..	CR	CR	..	CR	..
4	0	Kernick	2319	L.	—	—	—	....	....	xCS	xCS	....	CR	....
4	5	Great Treviscoe Siding	2230	L.	2	1	1	..	..	CR	CR	..	CR	..
4	18	Central Tréviscoe Siding	2231	126 F	—	—	—	....	....	CR	CR	....	CR	....
4	67	Parkandillack Siding	2232	189 F	—	—	—	..	..	CR	CR	..	CR	..
4	72	Stop Board	—	59 F	2	1	1	....	....	P	P	....	P	....
5	30	Whitegate Crossing ..	2233	51 F	2	1	1	..	..	—	—	..	CR	..
5	37	Whitegate Siding	2234	51 F	—	—	—	....	....	CR	CR	....	CR	....
6	29	Pochins Siding ..	2235	46 F	2	1	1	..	..	CR	CR	..	CR	..
7	1	**St. Dennis Junc.** arr.	2189	55 F	1	1	—	....	....	12 0	3 15	....	5 50	....

UP TRAINS. WEEK DAYS ONLY.

STATIONS.	Ruling Gradient 1 in	Time allowances for Ordinary Freight Trains (see page 2). Point to point times.	Allow for stop.	Allow for start.	1 K Mineral. RR	2 K Mineral. RR	3 K Mineral. RR	4	5 K Mineral. RR	6 K Mineral. RR
		Mins.	Mins.	Mins.	A.M.	A.M.	A.M.		P.M.	P.M.
St. Dennis Junc. dep.	....	—	—	1	6 50	....	10 35	....	....	1 15
Pochins Siding .	55 R	1	1	1	Will work as required on Branch.	..	CR	..	..	CR
Whitegate Siding	46 R	2	1	1		....	CR	....	....	CR
Whitegate Crossing ..	46 R	—	—	—		..	—	..	..	—
Parkandillack Siding	51 R	2	1	1		....	CS	..	....	CS
Central Treviscoe Siding	189 R	—	—	—		..	CR	..	..	CR
Great Treviscoe Siding	126 R	2	1	1		....	CR	....	....	CR
Kernick	L.	—	—	—		..	CSx	..	..	xCS
Trethosa Siding	L.	—	—	—		....	CR	....	....	CR
Little Treviscoe Siding	L.	1	1	1		..	CR	..	..	CR
Varcoe's & Goonv'nSdgs	L.	—	—	—		....	CR	....	....	CR
Slip Siding	40 R	—	—	—		..	CR	..	..	CR
Stop Board	40 R	2	1	1		....	P	....	....	P
Luke's New Siding ..	41 F	—	—	—		..	CR	..	..	CR
Luke's Old Siding	41 F	—	—	—		....	CR	....	....	CR
West of Eng. Co.'s Sdgs	41 F	—	—	—		..	CR	..	..	CR
Drinnick Mill	80 R	3	1	1	9 0	9 50	12 0	....	5 15	3 15
Wharf Line Siding	80 R	—	—	—		—	Min.	..	—	
Dubbers No. 1 Siding	80 R	—	—	—	..	—	K	....	—	....
Stop Board ..	80 R	2	1	1	..	P	A.M.	..	P	..
Carpella Sidings	50 F	—	—	—	....	—	11 50	....	CR	....
High Street Siding	48 F	3	1	1	...	P	CR	..	—	..
Stop Board	50 F	2	1	1	....	—	P	....	P	....
Langeth Crossing ..	50 F	—	—	—	..	—	—	..	—	..
Crugwallins Siding	50 F	—	—	—	..	—	CR	....	—	....
Burngullow West Sdg.	50 F	—	—	—	..	—	—	..	—	..
Burngullow arr.	50 F	3	1	—	....	10 20	12 10	...	5 54	....

All Down Trains must stop at Whitegate to pin down Brakes, if required.
When Empty or Loaded Trucks are taken from Little Treviscoe to Varcoes or Slip Siding they may be pushed by the Engine from Little Treviscoe.
Trucks for Whitegate Siding may be pushed by Engines of Up Trains from St. Dennis Junction to the Sidings, but the speed of the Train between those points must not exceed eight miles an hour.
When there are trucks at Drinnick Mill to be taken to Luke's Old Siding or to Luke's New Siding they may be pushed by the Engine from Drinnick Mill, but the speed of the Train must not exceed 8 miles an hour, and the Shunter must ride on the leading truck to keep a look out and give any necessary signal to the Driver.

September 1924

1951

Single Line, worked by Electric Train Staff. Crossing places, Kernick and Drinnick Mill.

Down Trains. Week Days only.

M.P. Mileage. M.	C.	Distance from Burngullow. M.	C.	STATIONS.	Ruling Gradient 1 in	Time Allowances for Ordinary Freight Trains. See page 6. Point to Point times.	Allow for Stop.	Allow for Start.	— Mineral. SO	K Mineral. SX	K Mineral. SX	K Mineral. SX
						Mins.	Mins.	Mins.	a.m.	a.m.	noon	p.m.
—	—	—	—	**BURNGULLOW** dep.	—	—	—	1	8 45	10 30	....	2 5
288	58	—	4	Burngullow West Sdg.	38 R.	—	—	—	—	—	..	—
288	68	—	17	Crugwallins Siding ..	50 R.	1	1	1	—	—	....	CR
289	28	—	58	Langeth Crossing ..	50 R.	—	—	—	—	—	..	—
—	—	—	—	Beacon Clay Siding ..	50 R.	—	—	—	—	—	....	—
290	0	1	24	High Street Siding ..	50 R.	8	1	1	CR	CR	..	CR
290	6	—	—	New Carpella Siding..	50 R.	—	—	—	9 0	10 45	....	—
291	29	2	53	Dubbers No. 1 Siding..	50 R.	5	1	1			..	—
291	31	2	55	Wharf Line Siding ..	L.	—	—	—	Extended to Drinnick Mill. RR	Extended to Drinnick Mill. RR	....	—
291	34	2	60	Drinnick Mill	L.	3	1	1			12 0	2 45
291	47	2	71	West of Eng. Co.'s Sdgs.	41 R.	—	—	—			CR	
291	63	3	7	Luke's Old Siding	41 R.	—	—	—			CR	....
—	—	3	26	Stop Board	41 R.	3	1	1			P	..
291	77	3	22	Luke's New Siding ..	40 F.	—	—	—			CR	....
—	—	3	30	Stop Board	40 F.	—	—	—			P	..
292	11	3	35	Slip Siding	40 F.	—	—	—	....	....	CR	....
292	21	3	45	Varcoe & Goonv'n Sdgs.	40 F.	1	1	1	..	..	CR	..
292	30	3	54	Little Treviscoe Siding	40 F.	—	—	—	....	....	CR	....
292	51	4	0	Kernick	L.	—	—	—	..	..	XCS	..
292	60	4	5	Great Treviscoe Siding	126 F.	2	1	1	....	....	CR	....
293	36	4	67	Parkandillack Siding..	59 F.	—	—	—	..	..	CR	..
—	—	4	72	Stop Board	256 F.	2	1	1	....	....	P	....
294	6	5	30	Whitegate Crossing ..	51 F.	2	1	1	..	..	—	..
294	13	5	37	Whitegate Siding ..	60 F.	—	—	—	....	....	CR	....
295	61	7	1	**ST. DENNIS JUNC.** arr.	55 F	1	1	—	..	..	1 5	..

Up Trains. Week Days only.

STATIONS.	Ruling Gradient 1 in	Time Allowances for Ordinary Freight Trains. See page 57. Point to Point times.	Allow for Stop.	Allow for Start.	K Mineral. SO	K Mineral. SX	K Mineral. SX	K Mineral. SX	K Mineral. SX
		Mins.	Mins.	Mins.	a.m.	a.m.	a.m.	a.m.	p.m.
ST. DENNIS JUNC. dep.	—	—	—	1	..	6 45	9 45	..	..
Whitegate Siding ..	55 R.	2	1	1	....	CR	CR	....	....
Whitegate Crossing ..	60. R.	—	—	—	..	—	—	..	..
Parkandillack Siding	51 R.	2	1	1	....	CR	CR	....	....
Great Treviscoe Siding	59 F.	2	1	1	..	CR	CR	..	..
Kernick	126 R.	—	—	—	....	CSX	CSX	....	....
Little Treviscoe Siding	L.	1	1	1	..	CR	CR	..	..
Varcoe's & Goonv'n Sds.	40 R.	—	—	—	....	CR	CR	....	....
Slip Siding	40 R.	—	—	—	..	CR	CR	..	..
Stop Board	40 R.	2	1	1	....	P	P	....	....
Luke's New Siding ..	40 R.	—	—	—	..	CR	CR	..	..
Luke's Old Siding	40 R.	—	—	—	....	CR	CR	....	....
West of Eng. Co.'s Sdgs.	41 F.	—	—	—	..	CR	CR	..	..
Drinnick Mill .. arr.	41 F.	3	1	1	....	7 30	10 50	....	....
Drinnick Mill .. dep.					..	9 40		..	4 10
Wharf Line Siding ..	L.	—	—	—	....	—	..	....	—
Dubbers No. 1 Siding..	L.	—	—	—	..	—	....	..	—
Stop Board	80 R.	2	1	1	....	P	..	....	P
New Carpella Sidings	50 F.	—	—	—	9 30	—	....	11 30	CR
High Street Siding....	50 F.	3	1	1	CR	—	..	CR	—
Stop Board	50 F.	2	1	1	P	P	....	P	P
Beacon Clay Siding....	50 F.	—	—	—	—	—	..	—	—
Langeth Crossing ..	50 F.	—	—	—	—	—	....	—	—
Crugwallins Siding....	50 F.	—	—	—	CR	—	..	CR	—
Burngullow West Sdg.	50 F.	—	—	—	—	—	....	—	—
BURNGULLOW arr.	38 F.	3	1	—	9 45	10 9	..	11 50	4 35

All Down Trains must stop at Whitegate to pin down Brakes, if required.
When Empty or Loaded Trucks are taken from Little Treviscoe to Varcoes or Slip Siding they may be pushed by the Engine from Little Treviscoe.
Trucks for Whitegate Siding may be pushed by Engines or Up Trains from St. Dennis Junction to the Sidings, but the speed of the Train between those points must not exceed 8 miles an hour.

BURNGULLOW

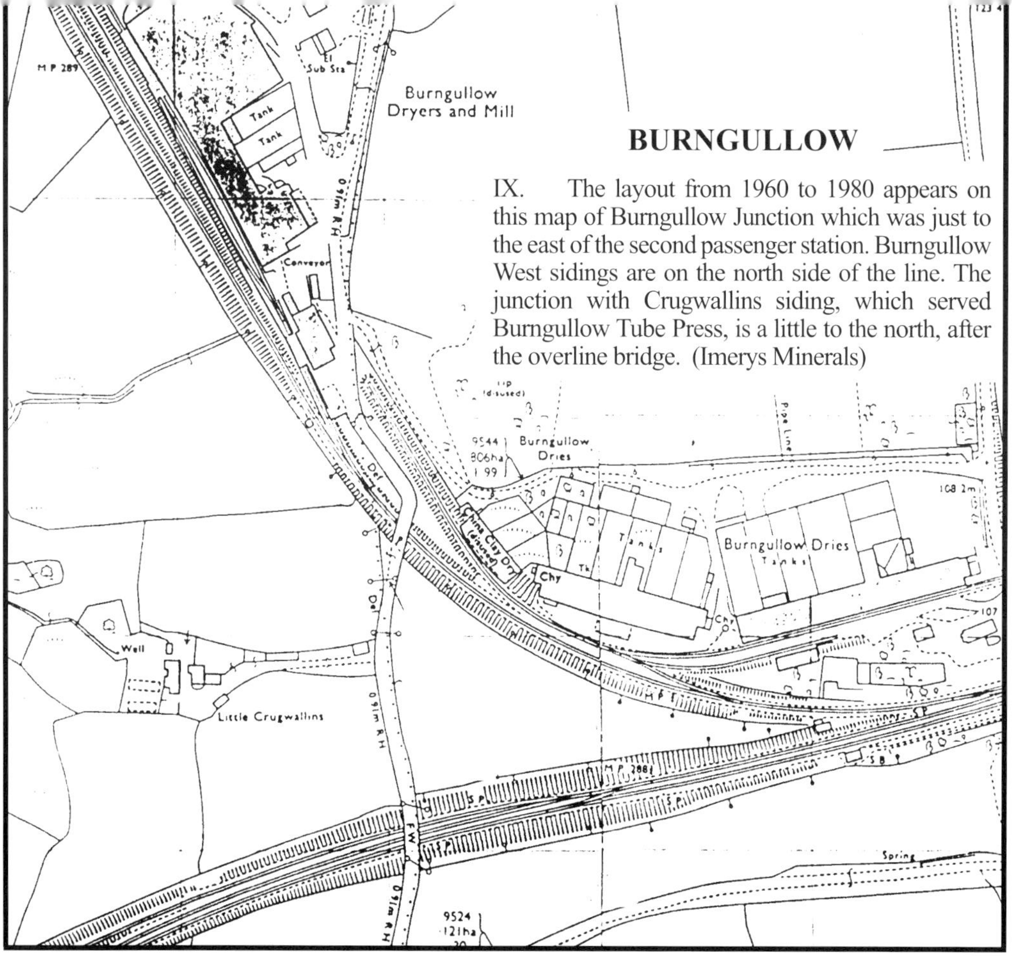

IX. The layout from 1960 to 1980 appears on this map of Burngullow Junction which was just to the east of the second passenger station. Burngullow West sidings are on the north side of the line. The junction with Crugwallins siding, which served Burngullow Tube Press, is a little to the north, after the overline bridge. (Imerys Minerals)

31. We look northwest on 22nd July 1991 as a train of polybulk wagons from Kernick, hauled by no.37671 *Tre Pol & Pen*, comes off the branch past the remains of the second Burngullow station. It will pass under the overline bridge to reach Blackpool sidings. (M.Dart)

BURNGULLOW WEST

32. Tehidy Minerals opened Burngullow West sidings a short distance around the curve from the junction. On 28th May 1989 we look west along the run round loop, alongside the overgrown siding which was closed in September 1974. (M.Dart)

CRUGWALLINS

33. ECC opened Crugwallins siding just beyond West Burngullow siding, on the up side, to serve a kiln, which was later utilised to house Burngullow tube press. This view looks north along the siding on 13th September 1995. 0-4-0DH no.P403D *Denise* is hauling empty CDA wagons towards the loading area. After loading they will be propelled on to the loop for collection by a main line locomotive. (M.Dart)

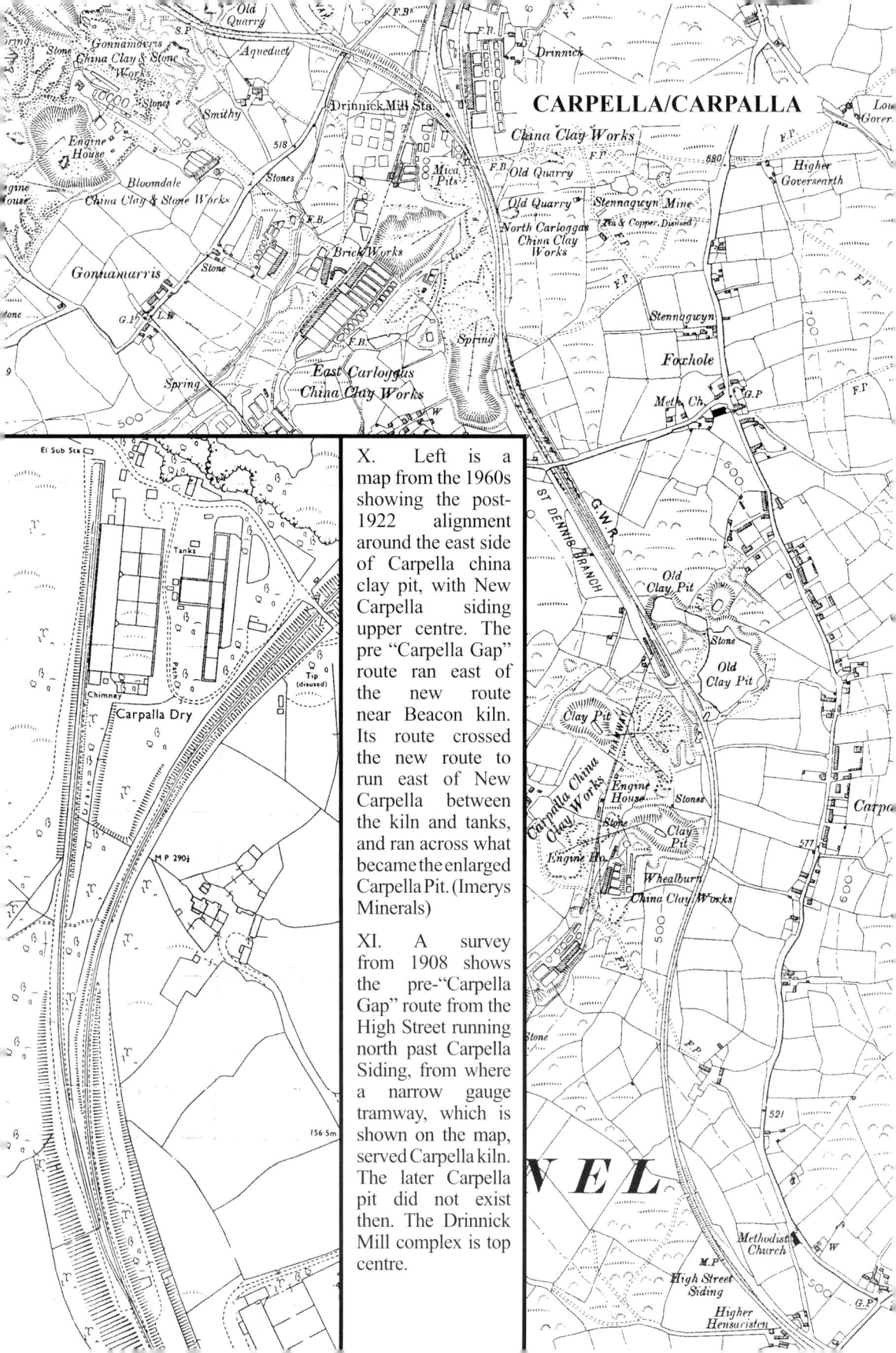

X. Left is a map from the 1960s showing the post-1922 alignment around the east side of Carpella china clay pit, with New Carpella siding upper centre. The pre "Carpella Gap" route ran east of the new route near Beacon kiln. Its route crossed the new route to run east of New Carpella between the kiln and tanks, and ran across what became the enlarged Carpella Pit. (Imerys Minerals)

XI. A survey from 1908 shows the pre-"Carpella Gap" route from the High Street running north past Carpella Siding, from where a narrow gauge tramway, which is shown on the map, served Carpella kiln. The later Carpella pit did not exist then. The Drinnick Mill complex is top centre.

34. After Lanjeth level crossing there were sidings on the up side at Beacon and at High Street that served loading wharves. We look north at the pre "Carpella Gap" alignment on 28th May 1989. The track on this short section was retained as a headshunt for High Street siding. (M.Dart)

35. A further siding was opened at New Carpella by the Carpella United China Clay Co; it was on the down side of the new alignment. From there the new route swung around the east side of Carpella clay pit and entered a cutting. This is spanned by a pipeline and a bridge, which are shown in this north facing view on 28th May 1989. (M.Dart)

DRINNICK MILL/NANPEAN WHARF

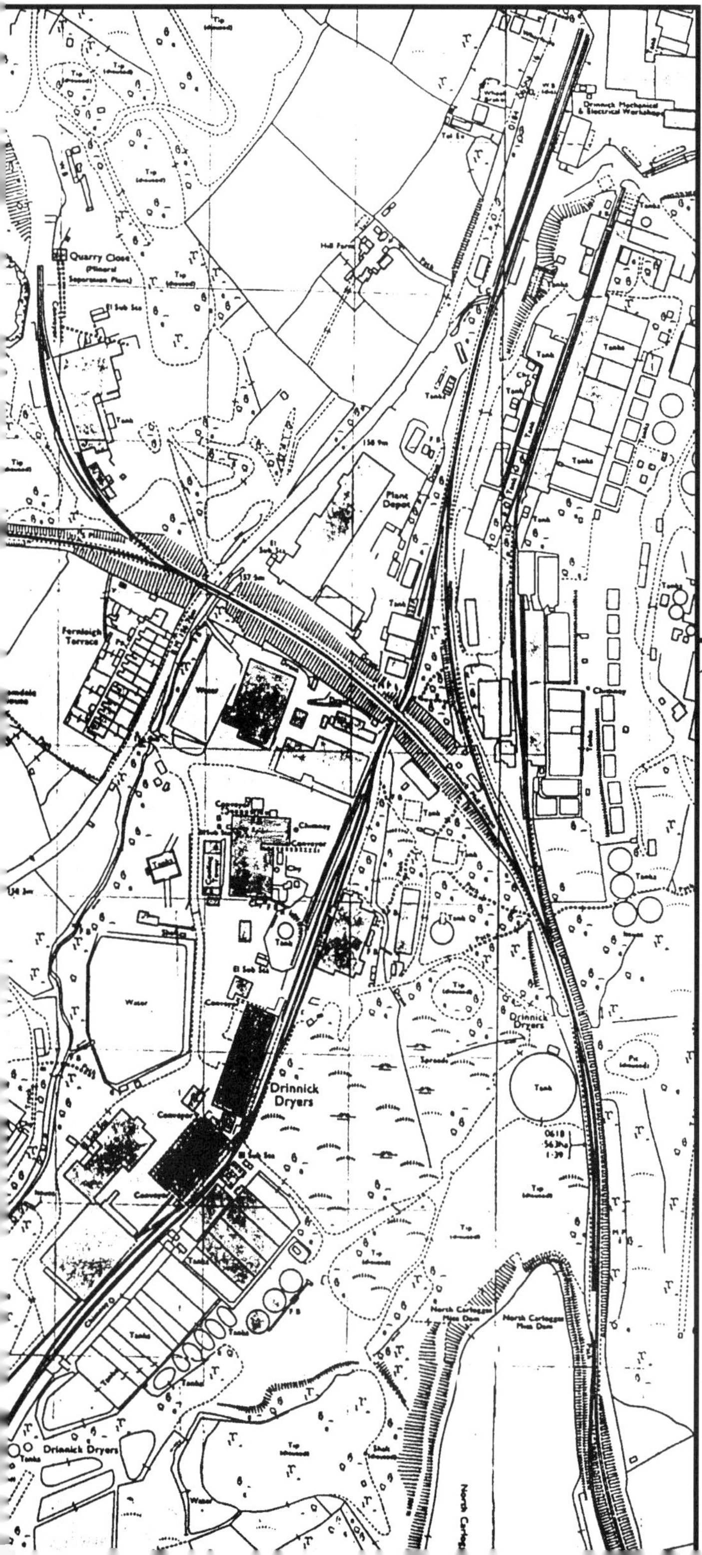

XII. A map from the 1960s shows the branch lower right with Dubbers no.1 siding diverging to the right. The line to Nanpean Wharf and Dubbers no.2 siding diverged north, as the main branch curved west. The low level lines climbed to pass below the main branch, and joined the line to Nanpean Wharf. West of England Cos. siding to Quarry Close diverged north on the west side of the map. Drinnick Mill station was in the fork of the main branch and Nanpean Wharf lines. (Imerys Minerals)

XIII. This shows the revised layout on the low level lines, following the replacement of coal fired kilns by mechanical dryers. This layout still exists, but the rails have become buried under sand in places. (M.Dart/ Branch Line Society)

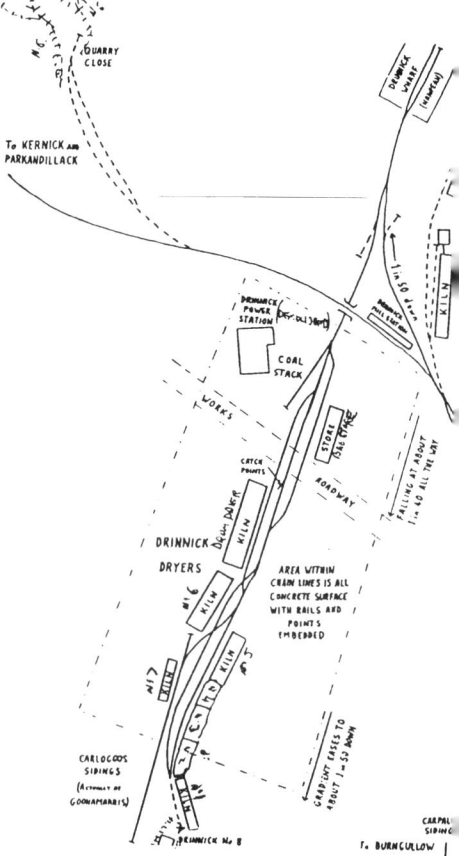

36. Beyond Carpella pit came Carpella siding, which was opened by the Carpella China Clay Co. The line continued through a cutting to approach Drinnick Mill. In 1939, a loop was provided on the down side south of the complex and in 1966 it was truncated to form a siding. After the loop came Dubbers no.2 siding which is on the left as we look south east in the 1930s. An elderly pannier tank with a couple of wagons is on the line from Drinnick Mill. (Imerys Minerals)

37. Looking north at Drinnick Mill on 17th June 1977 we find no.25217 on a train of sheeted open wagons loaded with clay. From right to left are the trackbed of Dubbers no.2 siding, the line diverging to Nanpean Wharf and Drinnick Mill control building. This was demolished on 1st October 1993. Next left are two bridges; the first crossed over the low level lines and is seen between the telegraph poles. Further to the left, the second bridge crossed the road from Nanpean to Treviscoe. (T.Heavyside)

38. We look north on 1st October 1955 along the line which dropped at 1 in 50 from Drinnick Mill to Nanpean Wharf. Wagons on the right are on Dubbers no.1 siding and on the left the low level line joins the Nanpean Wharf line. (M.Dart)

39. We look north and witness activity at Nanpean Wharf in June 1958. Previously called Drinnick Mill, it was a public goods station. 0-6-0PT no. 9755 is propelling wagons into one of the loading bays. (N. Simmons/H.Davies photos)

40. A similar view on 15th May 1999 shows the Wharf being used for storing small clay slurry tank wagons awaiting scrapping. During the 1990s calcified seaweed was loaded here. New development is apparent on the right. (M.Dart)

CARLOGGOS/DRINNICK LOW LEVEL LINES

41. A view from the 1930s looks west across the low level lines which fall on a gradient that is steeper than 1 in 40. The lines are below the grassy bank. The wagons are on a siding that served coal drops at Drinnick power station. Demolition took place in the 1990s. (Imerys Minerals)

42. We look north east up the low level lines from Drinnick nos.5,6,7 and 8 kilns towards Nanpean Wharf. No.37673 is running down the incline to collect a loaded wagon from Drinnick no.7 on 14th May 1992. A Tiger wagon is in the distance on the left. It had a cracked frame and is on the power station siding. The bridge carrying the main branch is in the distance. (M.Dart)

43. This is a south westerly view taken near the bottom end of the low level lines in the early 1920s. Sidings, which served some of the old Drinnick kilns and North Carloggos clay works are in the distance. (Mr Lillicrap snr/M.Dart coll.)

44. We look north east from Drinnick no.7 kiln on 14th May 1992. No.37673 has departed with the last polybulk wagon to be loaded there, and is heading up the low level lines past a derelict clay mill on the right and Drinnick no.6 kiln on the left. (M.Dart)

45. On the same day no.37673 was inside the covered loading area alongside the linhay of Drinnick no 7 Buell dryer; it was coupling to the last traffic from there by rail. The line extended beyond the dryer to a shunting neck at North Carloggos. The line on the left crossed a bridge over a stream to reach Drinnick no 8 kiln. (M.Dart)

46. Drinnick no. 8 is featured in this south facing view from the 1950s. We see a narrow gauge tramway each side of the siding; skip wagons ran on this to carry clay from the linhay to standard gauge trucks, which are seen sheeted over. (Mr Lillicrap snr/M.Dart coll.)

47. The line from Drinnick Mill to St.Dennis junction crossed the road from Nanpean to Treviscoe. This view from 30th October 1991, looks north east and shows no.37671 *Tre Pol & Pen* heading for Parkandillack with an inspection saloon. (M.Dart)

WEST OF ENGLAND CO SIDING/QUARRY CLOSE

48. Immediately after the branch had crossed the bridge seen in the previous picture, West of England Co siding diverged on the up side. It served china stone works. China stone was brought to the loading area by 2ft gauge tramways. This scene from the early 1930s looks north east. We see an elderly 0-6-0PT moving a loaded train out of the siding towards Drinnick Mill. This siding was known locally as "Capn Brewers" (Imerys Minerals)

GOONVEAN/RESTOWRACK

49. As the line climbed at 1 in 50 through a cutting, Cathedral Quarry was on the up side, followed by Lukes Old and Lukes New sidings on the down side. The line passed through Slip bridge which we see as we look east on 28th May 1989. Slip siding followed on the down side. It served a china stone quarry which possessed two Blondin aerial ropeways. Restowrack siding was on the up side near the sandy area in the centre of the picture. Goonvean siding, which converged on the down side, is on the right in the picture. Varcoes siding was between Goonvean siding and the main branch. (M.Dart)

50. From its junction with the main branch, Goonvean siding curved around and split into two lines to serve a pair of kilns. Rails remained buried beneath clay in this south easterly facing view from 28th May 1989. A narrow gauge tramway ran from the end of the siding to South Goonvean kiln. (M.Dart)

51. We look north from the end of Goonvean siding on 17th June 1989. A flat truck remained despite the siding having closed in January 1976, it was used as a bridge between two buildings. (M.Dart)

LITTLE TREVISCOE

52. After Goonvean siding, Little Treviscoe siding converged on the down side. It was served by a narrow gauge tramway which tunnelled beneath the road and ended beneath the linhay of Bowser kiln. Shortly after this, the line passed over Little Treviscoe ungated level crossing which was renewed in 1993. We look west on 25th November 1993 as no.37673 approaches the crossing with loaded air braked stock for Stoke-on-Trent. (M.Dart)

TRETHOSA

53. Trethosa siding that followed next and converged on the down side, is featured in this 1930s south facing scene. It was removed to permit expansion of Trethosa pit. (Mr Lillicrap snr/M.Dart coll.)

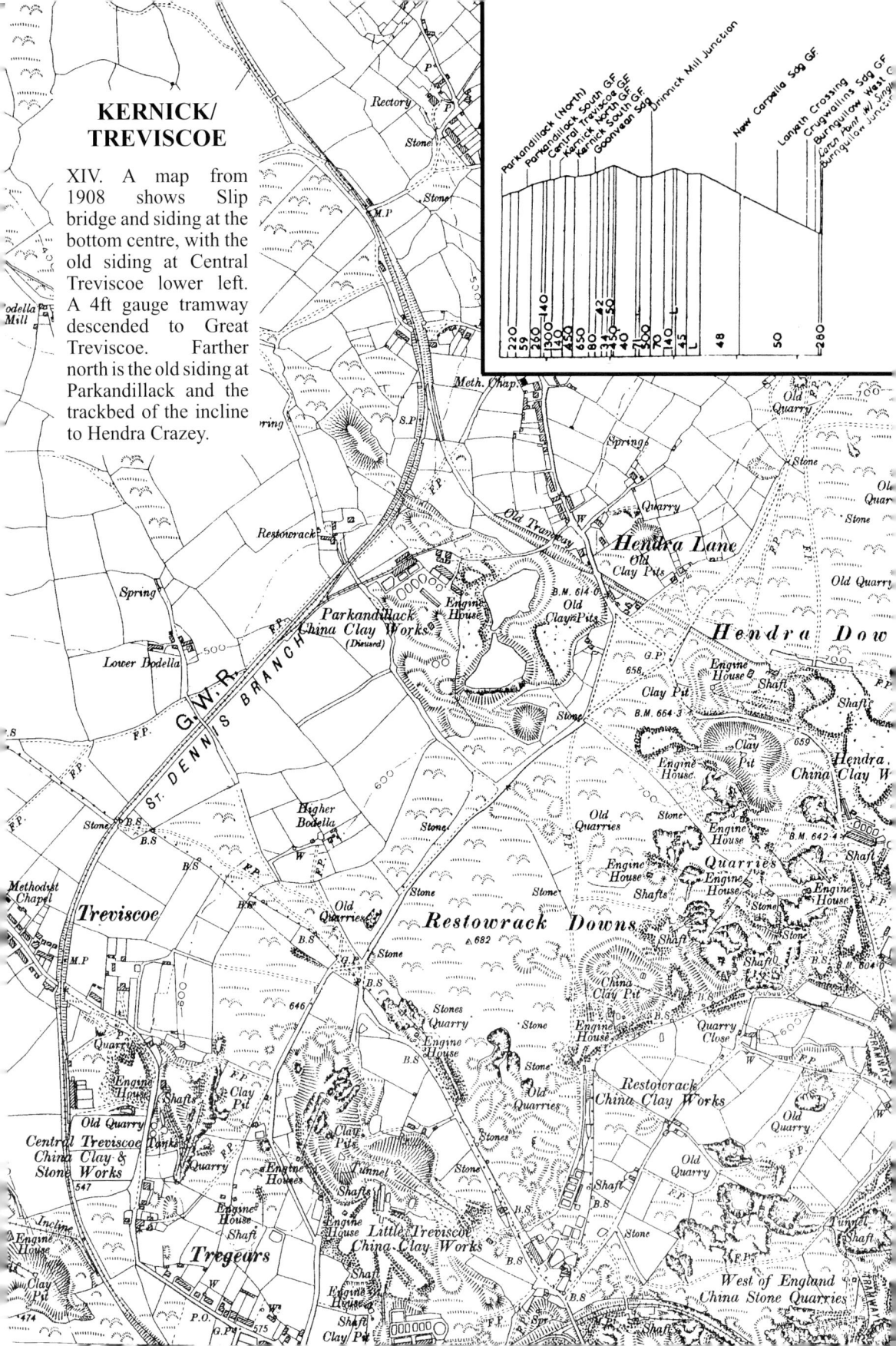

KERNICK/ TREVISCOE

XIV. A map from 1908 shows Slip bridge and siding at the bottom centre, with the old siding at Central Treviscoe lower left. A 4ft gauge tramway descended to Great Treviscoe. Farther north is the old siding at Parkandillack and the trackbed of the incline to Hendra Crazey.

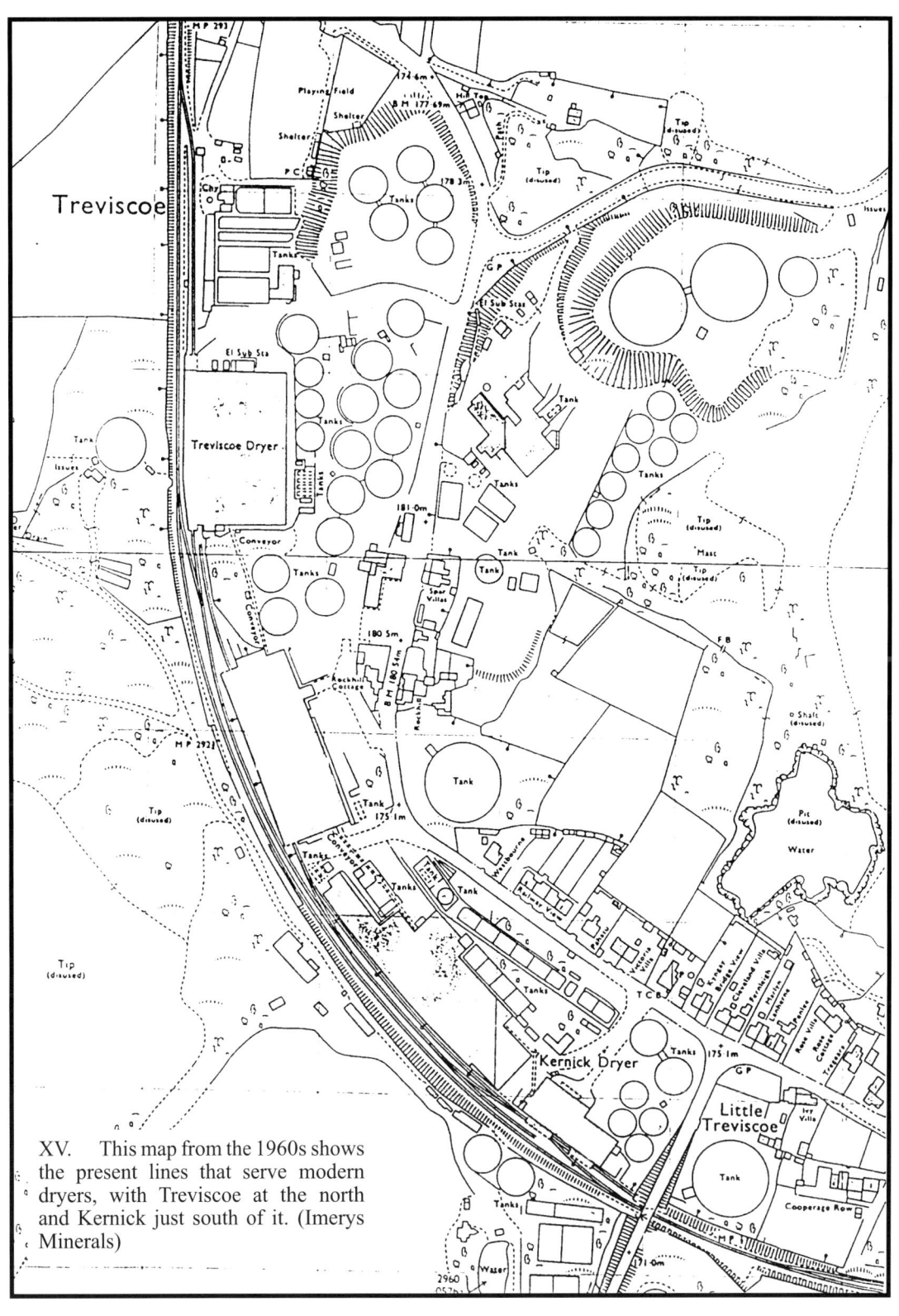

XV. This map from the 1960s shows the present lines that serve modern dryers, with Treviscoe at the north and Kernick just south of it. (Imerys Minerals)

54. We pass under Kernick bridge to Kernick siding where, on 26th March 2002, no.66189 is coupled to Polybulk wagons ready to depart to St.Blazey. As we look north we see the site of Great Treviscoe siding to the left of centre. From there, a tramway, which was laid on stone blocks, descended the hillside from a loading wharf to a kiln. (M.Dart)

55. Here we look south east to Kernick siding in the early 1920s, where a variety of private owner wagons await loading. The line was extended to the left by ECC to form Treviscoe siding. (Imerys Minerals)

56.   We look north inside the loading area at Central Treviscoe which continues north from Kernick and Treviscoe. A siding which had existed here had been closed and the present siding was laid for ECC. Trackmobile 95TM no.P404D Elaine is positioning CDA wagons for loading on a very wet 26th February 1992. This road/rail machine was used to shunt wagons at the Treviscoe/Kernick complex. The main drive was to the rail wheels. (M. Dart)

57.   Looking south at Kernick North on 1st August 2000, no.66220 has dropped off empty CDA wagons and is preparing to take the remainder to Parkandillack. (M.Dart)

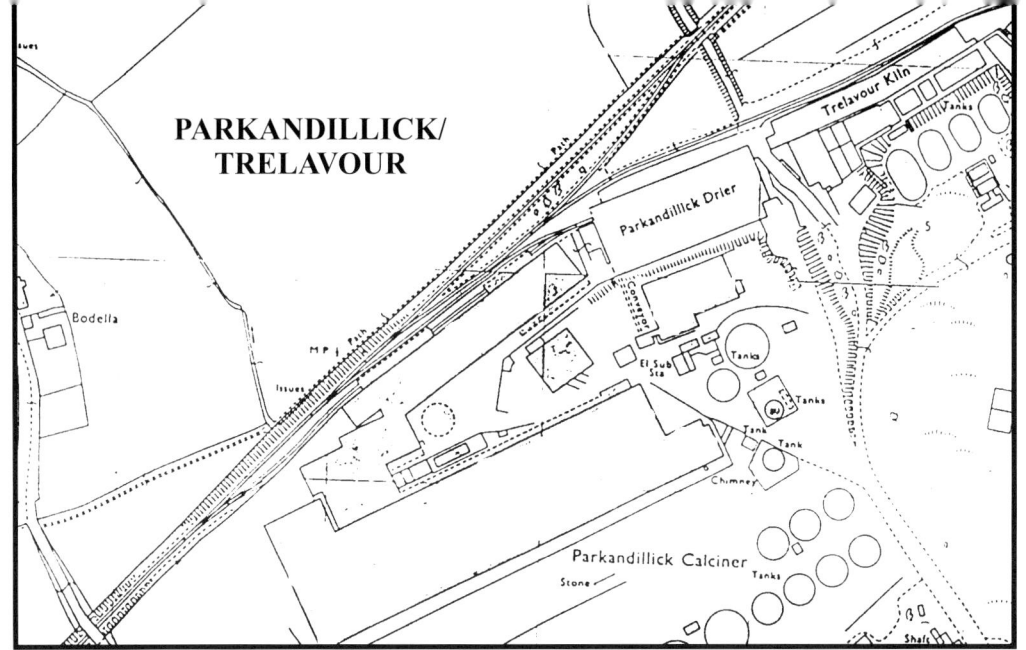

XVI. A map from the 1970s of Parkandillack and Trelavour shows the present day layout with the calciner at the south end, the Buell dryer in the centre and the truncated branch.(Imerys Minerals)

58. The line descended at 1 in 50/40 from Treviscoe to Parkandillack, where the line now terminates. The layout here was remodelled in 1925, 1958 and 1972. We look north east on 1st June 1994 to see no.37229 with polybulk wagons at the loading area for Molochite, which is a refractory. The loading area for the Buell dryer is out of view behind the train. (M.Dart)

59. Still looking northeast on 9th March 1994 we are further along the siding. No.37521 waits for wagons to be loaded at the new Buell site. (M.Dart)

60. Between the siding to the new Buell dryer and the end of the main branch, a siding ran north east to serve Trelavour kiln. This was owned by the Goonvean & Restowrack China Clay Co. This rare photo depicts no.56013 carrying out clearance trials at Trelavour on 27th February 1990. It had been a day of torrential rain when the sun only appeared for five minutes, luckily at this location. (M.Dart)

61. Now we look northwest at Parkandillack on 30th October 1991 to see no.37671 *Tre Pol & Pen*. It has run around inspection saloon no.DB99506 and is waiting to return to St.Blazey. The branch terminated shortly after the points where the loop rejoined the line. Trelavour siding diverged to the right. (M.Dart)

DOMELLICK

62. After Parkandillack, the Hendra incline joined the up side just before Whitegates level crossing and siding at St.Dennis, where there was a loading wharf. The line continued in a shallow cutting which was crossed by a bridge which carried a farm track. It is shown in this view which looks north on 2nd May 1995. After a third of a mile the line passed below Domellick bridge, which carried the road from St.Dennis to Indian Queens. (M.Dart)

POCHINS SIDING

63. A quarter of a mile beyond Domellick bridge, the route passed Pochins siding which was also known as Gothers, Domellick or Melangoose. A tramway ended on the loading wharf, which we see as we look southeast on 12th June 1989. It ran across the Goss Moor for over two miles from Gothers/Wheal Frederick china clay works near Enniscaven. (M.Dart)

ST. DENNIS JUNCTION/BODMIN ROAD JUNCTION

64. We look southeast at St.Dennis Junction on 1st October 1955. 2-6-2T no.4526 is running around the stock of a Plymouth Railway Circle brake van special, that had arrived from Burngullow. 0-6-0PT no.3705 is bringing a train off the Retew branch which the special train traversed later. (M.Dart)

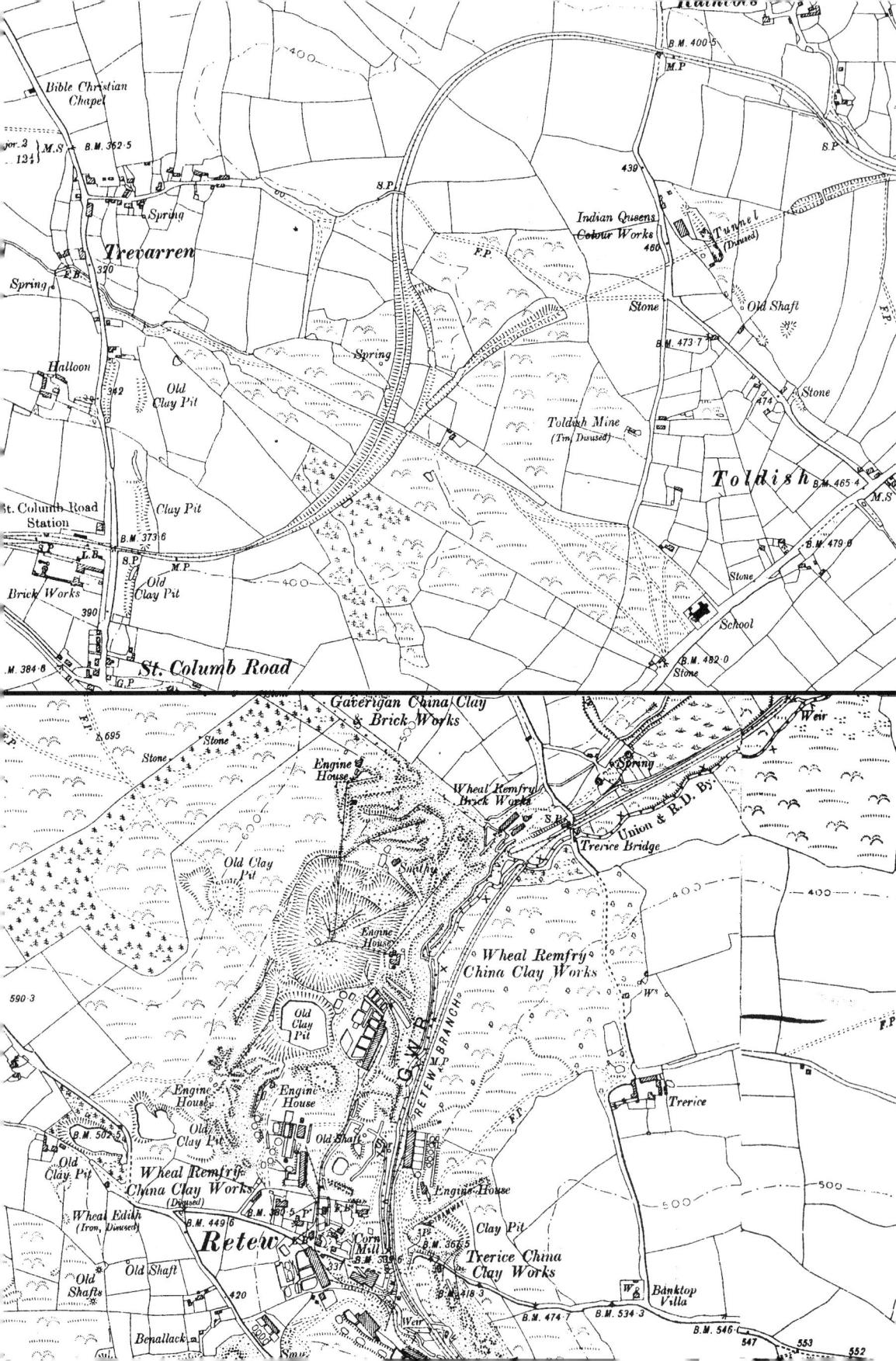

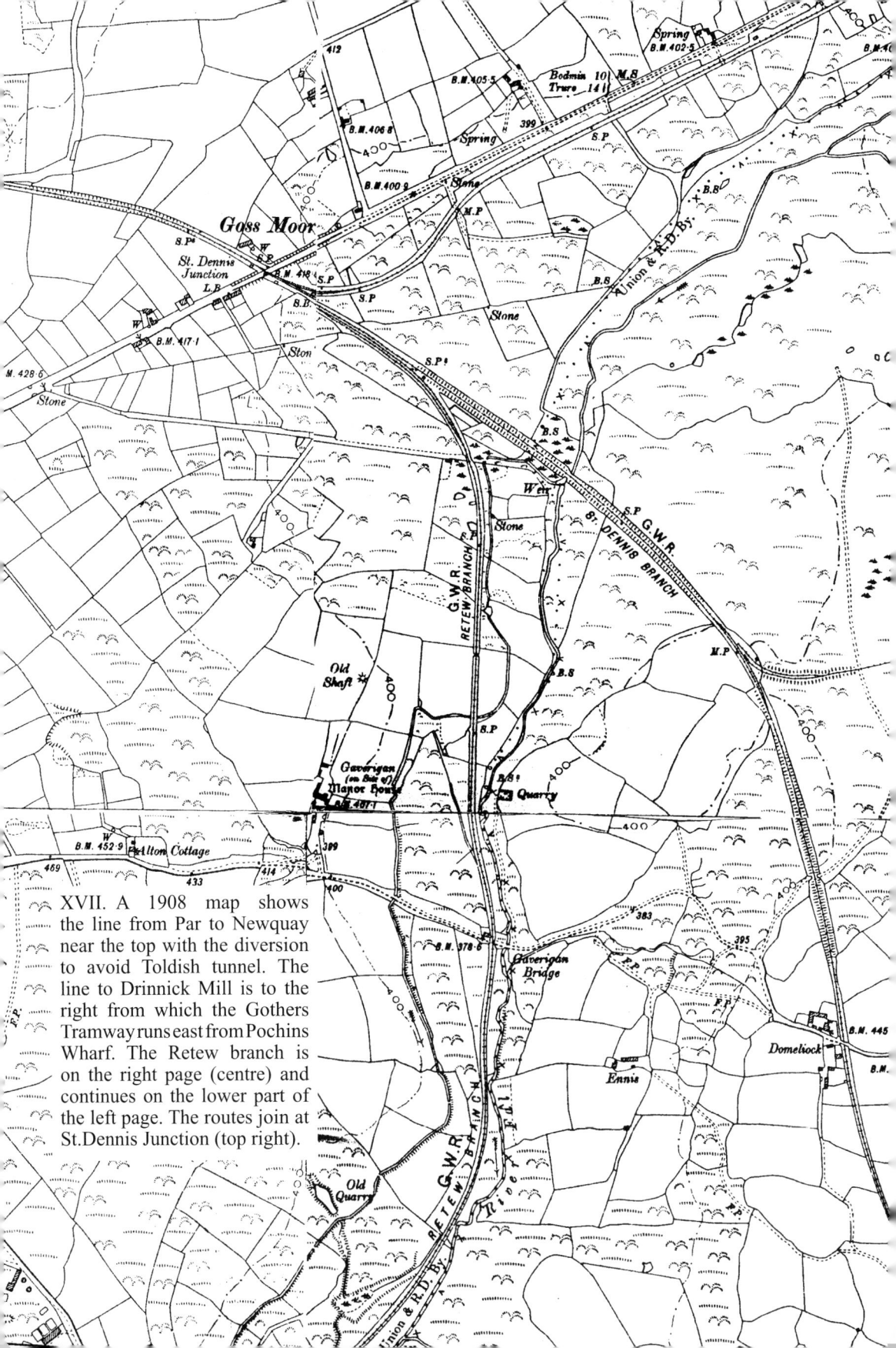

XVII. A 1908 map shows the line from Par to Newquay near the top with the diversion to avoid Toldish tunnel. The line to Drinnick Mill is to the right from which the Gothers Tramway runs east from Pochins Wharf. The Retew branch is on the right page (centre) and continues on the lower part of the left page. The routes join at St. Dennis Junction (top right).

65. Looking north west at St.Dennis Junction in June 1958 we see 0-6-0PT no.9755 stopped near the signal box during shunting movements. A train from Par, hauled by a 2-6-2T, is heading to Newquay. (N. Simmons/H.Davies photos.)

Further photographs appear in the *Branch Lines to Newquay* and *St.Austell to Penzance* volumes.

66. A few lines were retained at the St.Dennis Junction end of the branch. Following problems with newly introduced CDA wagons, a facility for cleaning their interiors was installed by the remaining sidings. Later this site was utilised for removing the interior plastic lining from CDA wagons. It had been breaking up and causing contamination of the clay. We look south east along the yard on 30th November 1990 as no.37674 drops off a rake of wagons for lining removal. It will return with other wagons to St.Blazey. (M.Dart)

67. When the Indian Queens bypass was constructed, a new bridge was built to carry it over the Newquay line at St.Dennis junction. Provision was made for a connection from the branch to be restored if required. Looking southeast we view the bridge on 24th April 1997. The line from Newquay to Par curves left to cross Goss Moor. All of the lines in the yard have been removed. (M.Dart)

7. RETEW BRANCH-ST.DENNIS JUNCTION TO MELEDOR MILL

This line served china clay and brick works in the Fal valley. There were public goods stations at Melangoose Mill and Meledor Mill. The CMR's Act, mentioned earlier, permitted this line, known as the Retew branch, to be constructed. It ran from Bodmin Road (later St.Dennis) Junction to Melangoose Mill and was opened on 1st June 1874. In 1883 a short narrow gauge tramway was laid to Meledor works. This was replaced in 1886 by a standard gauge siding, that was extended southwards on the trackbed of another narrow gauge tramway, for a quarter mile to Virginia china clay kiln. Further tramways ran from here to Burgotha kiln and an old air dry at West Virginia. A GWR Act of 26th July 1910 enabled the Retew branch extension to be built southwards to Meledor Mill. It opened on 1st July 1912 and ran over the route of the siding to Virginia for the first quarter of a mile. On 11th October 1921 a further extension was opened. This passed over a fully gated level crossing to serve the Cornish Meledor China Clay Co. The branch closed on 3rd April 1982.

OPENING AND CLOSING DATES OF SIDINGS

	Opened	Closed
Gaverigan	NA	6th February 1966
Trerice	NA	15th April 1966
MacLarens	9th April 1924	20th March 1966
New Trerice	22nd March 1911	13th March 1966
Retew	6th October 1882	1972
South Fraddon	5th December 1939	1973
New Halwyn	26th April 1912	20th March 1966
Wheal Benallick	1st January 1906	June 1973
Melangoose Mill	1st June 1874	June 1973
Grove	1st May 1886	1964
Virginia	1886	March 1965
West Treviscoe	1st July 1912	5th March 1965
Tolbenny	19th June 1931	1972
Burgotha	10th October 1921	1972
Melbur	21st February 1918	3rd April 1982
Meledor Mill	1st July 1912	3rd April 1982
New Meledor	11th October 1921	3rd April 1982

June 1879

Down Trains.					Up Trains.				
Distances from Melangoose Siding	STATIONS.	Goods and Minerals.			Distances from St. Dennis Junctn.	STATIONS.	Goods and Minerals.		
		arr	Pass	dep				¾ dep	
		R|R	p.m.				R|R	noon.	
—	Melangoose Sg.	...	12 20	...	—	St. Dennis Jnc.	...	12 0	...
¼	Retew Siding	C|R		...	2	Trerice Siding	C|R		...
¾	Trerice Siding	C|R		...	2½	Retew Siding	C|R		...
2¾	St. Dennis Jnc.	12 30		...	2¾	Melangoose ,,	12 10		...

July 1910

Up Trains.						Down Trains.					
Distance from Melangoose Siding	STATIONS.	1 Minerals.	2 Minerals.	3 Minerals.	4 Minerals.	STATIONS.	1 Minerals.	2 Minerals.	3 Minerals.	4 Minerals.	
		dep.	dep.	dep.	dep.		arr dep.	arr dep.	dep. dep.	dep.	
M C		A.M. R|R	A.M. R|R	P.M. R|R	P.M. R|R		A.M. R|R	A.M. R|R	P.M. R|R	P.M. R|R	
— —	Melangoose Sdg.	9 0	11 15	3 5	5 0	St. Dennis Jn. s.s.	— 8 15	— 10 30	2 25	4 15	
— —	Anchor Clay Co.s Sdg	C|R	C|R	C|R	C|R	Gaverigan Crossing	—	—	—	—	
0 35	Retew Siding	9 5	11 20	C|R	C|R	Trerice Crossing	—	—	—	—	
0 42	Trerice New Siding	C|R	C|R	C|R	C|R	Trerice Siding	C|R	C|R	C|R	C|R	
0 75	Trerice Siding	C|R		C|R	C|R	Trerice New Siding	C|R	C|R	C|R	C|R	
0 75	Trerice Crossing	—	—	—	—	Retew Siding	8 25 8 37	10 40 10 42	2 37	C|R	
1 60	Gaverigan Crossing	—	—	—	—	Anchor Clay Co.'s Siding	C|R	C|R	C|R	C|R	
2 50	St. Dennis Jn. s.s.	9 15	11 30	3 20	5 15	Melangoose Sdg.	8 30	10 45	2 40	4 30	

All Trains must stop at Retew Siding for the Guard to put the Points right.

September 1924

DOWN TRAINS.		1 Minerals.	2 Minerals.	3 Minerals.	4	Distance from Meledor Siding	UP TRAINS.	Station No.	1 Minerals.	2 Minerals.	3 Minerals.	4
		arr dep.	arr dep.	dep.		M C			dep.	dep.	dep.	
		A.M. A.M. R|R	A.M. A.M. R|R	P.M. R|R					A.M. R|R	A.M. R|R	P.M. R|R	
St. Dennis Jn. s.s		— 8 30	— 10 30	2 25	...	— —	Meledor Mill N. Sidings.	2317	9 30	11 13	3 17	...
Gaverigan Crossing		—	—	—	...	0 04	West Treviscoe	2322	C|R	C|R	C|R	...
Trerice Crossing		—	—	—	...	1 12	Virginia Siding	2316	C|R	C|R	C|R	...
Trerice Siding		C|R	C|R	C|R	...		Melangoose Mill Siding	2242	9 40	11 23	3 25	...
Trerice New Siding		C|R	C|R	C|R	...	1 23	Anchor Clay Co's Sdg	2241	C|R	C|R	C|R	...
Retew Siding		C|R	10 40 10 42	2 37	...	1 28	Retew Siding	2240	9 42	11 30	C|R	...
AnchorClayCo's Sdg		C|R	C|R	C|R	...	1 42	New Howlyn		—	—	—	...
Melangoose Mill		C|R	10 45 10 50	2 40	...	1 49	Trerice New Siding	2239	C|R	C|R	C|R	...
Virginia Siding		C|R	C|R	C|R	...	2 12	Trerice Siding	2238	C|R	—	C|R	...
Stop Board		P	P	P	...	2 20	Trerice Crossing	2237	—	—	—	...
West Treviscoe		C|R	C|R	C|R	...	3 4	Gaverigan Crossing	2236	—	—	—	...
Meledor Mill N Sidings.		9 0 —	10 55	2 50	...	3 74	St. Dennis Jn. s.s	2189	9 55	11 40	3 40	...

1951

Down Trains.					Week Days only.		Up Trains.				
M.P. Mileage.	STATIONS	Ruling Gradient 1 in	K Mineral.	K Mineral. SX	K Mineral. SX	STATIONS	Ruling Gradient 1 in	K Mineral.	K Mineral. SX	K Mineral. SX	
M. C.			dep. a.m.	dep. p.m.	dep. p.m.			dep. a.m.	dep. p.m.	dep. p.m.	
— —	ST. DENNIS JCT.	—	8 15	12 45	4 50	MELEDOR MILL N. Sds.	—	11 15	3 15	8 10	
0 70	Gaverigan Crossing	104 F	—	—	—	Tolbenny Siding	95 R	C|R	C|R	—	
1 55	Trerice Crossing	202 F	—	—	—	West Treviscoe	65 R	C|R	C|R	—	
1 56	Trerice Siding	223 F	C|R	C|R	—	Virginia Siding	40 R	C|R	C|R	C|R	
1 72	McLaren's Siding N.	149 F	C|R	C|R	—	MELANGOOSE MILL	40 R	11 25	3 25	C|R	
2 4	Trerice New Siding	149 F	C|R	C|R	—	Anchor Clay Co.'s Sdg	40 R	C|R	C|R	—	
2 34	New Halwyn	60 F	C|R	C|R	—	Retew Siding	115 R	11 30	C|R	C|R	
2 36	Retew Siding	60 F	C|R	1 5	5‡25	New Halwyn	60 R	—	—	—	
2 55	Anchor Clay Co.'s Sdg.	115 F	C|R	C|R	—	Trerice New Siding	60 R	C|R	C|R	—	
2 63	MELANGOOSE MILL	40 F	CRP	1P15	5‡45P	McLaren's Siding N.	149 R	C|R	C|R	—	
2 69	Virginia Siding	40 F	C|R	C|R	—	Trerice Siding	149 R	C|R	—	—	
3 5	West Treviscoe	40 F	C|R	C|R	—	Trerice Crossing	223 R	—	—	—	
3 44	Tolbenny Siding	65 F	C|R	C|R	—	Gaverigan Crossing	202 R	—	—	—	
3 67	MELEDOR MILL N Sds.	95 F	9 15	1 20	5 55	ST. DENNIS JCT.	104 R	11 50	3 50	6 50	

‡—Arrive 5.10 p.m.   ‡—Arrive 5.35 p.m.

XVIII. This portion of a 2½ ins to the mile map of 1938 shows the complete Retew branch from St. Dennis Junction to Meledor Mill with the extension over the road to Collins. The original terminus at Melangoose Mill is just to the east of Halwyn. The St. Dennis Junction to Trethosa section of the line to Drinnick Mill is shown on the right.

ST DENNIS JUNCTION

68. We look southeast on 1st October 1955 as 0-6-0PT no.3705 brings a train of loaded clay wagons off the Retew branch. The line to Drinnick Mill is on the left. (M.Dart)

TRERICE

69. South of St.Dennis Junction, on the up side, was Gaverigan siding, which formed a loop. Next came Gaverigan level crossing. Trerice level crossing and siding followed this. This was formerly called Wheal Remfry brick works siding and was on the up side. McLarens (Wheal Remfry) siding followed on the down side. Next, also on the down side, was New Trerice (Trewheela) siding which we see as we look south on 31st May 1966. (M.Dart)

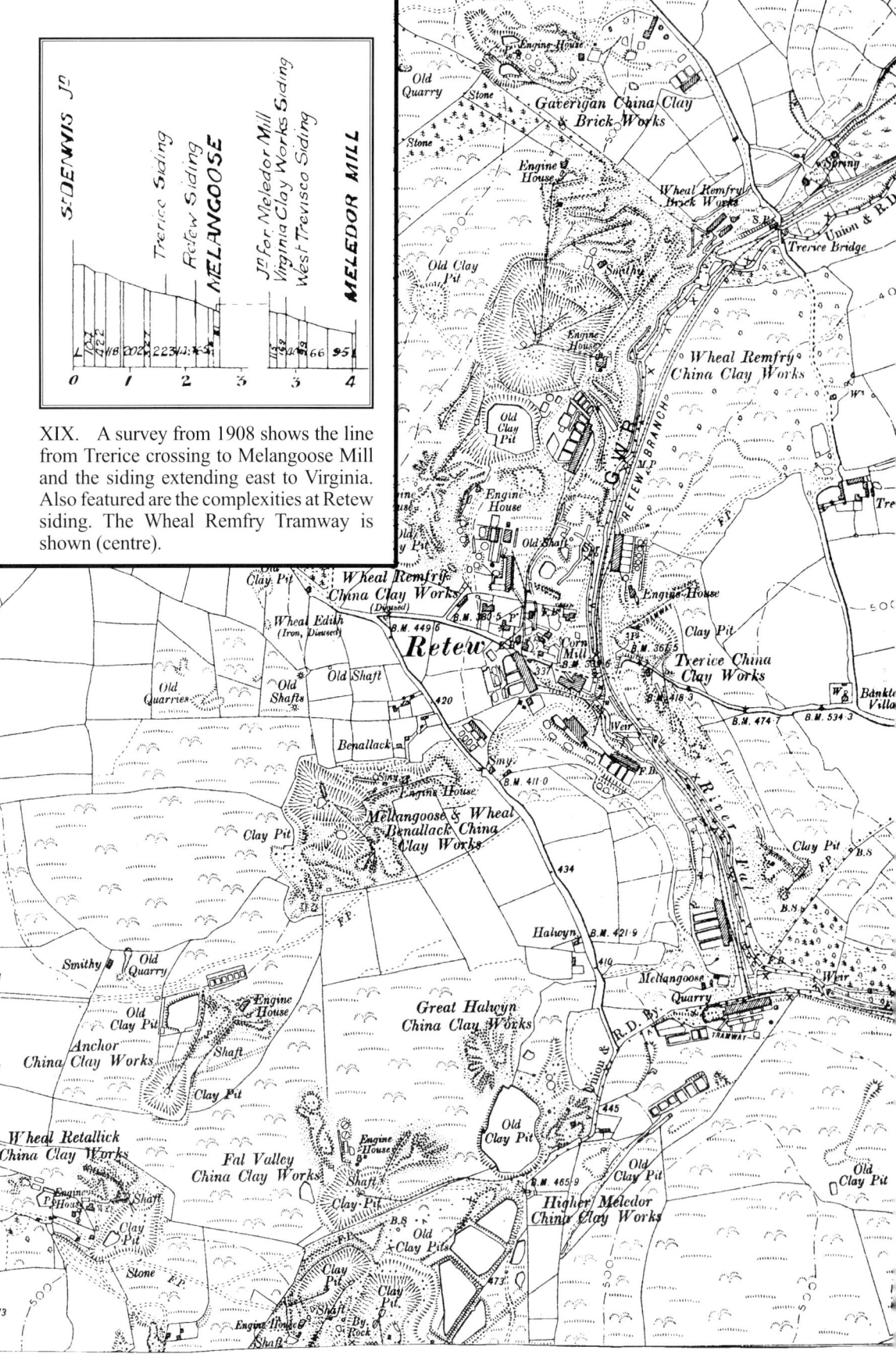

XIX. A survey from 1908 shows the line from Trerice crossing to Melangoose Mill and the siding extending east to Virginia. Also featured are the complexities at Retew siding. The Wheal Remfry Tramway is shown (centre).

RETEW

70.   Retew (Fal Valley) siding branched off on the up side, just before the main branch passed over Retew level crossing. This siding curved away and split into two lines. Both of these crossed bridges over the River Fal and one of the lines is seen in this view which looks southeast on 31st May 1966. (M.Dart)

71.   Beyond the bridge over the River Fal, the southernmost part of Retew siding split into two forks which served differently aligned kilns. We look north on 19th May 1968 along the southern section. At one time a connection had existed from the south fork to the north fork and this had formed a small triangle. This had disappeared beneath brambles and the whole area has been buried beneath clay works debris. (M. Dart)

SOUTH FRADDON/DRY KILN

72. This siding diverged just after Retew level crossing on the down side. It climbed to reach the kiln which is concealed by trees in this southeast view from 31st May 1966. The track laid in concrete still remains. The main branch can be seen descending on the right. (M.Dart)

NEW HALWYN

73. As this siding diverged on the up side, Retew Loop commenced on the down side. We look south at both of these on 31st May 1966. (M. Dart)

MELANGOOSE MILL

74. Wheal Benallick (Anchor) siding came next on the up side. It leads off to the right in this view, which looks south on 31st May 1966. The lines in the centre ran to Melangoose Mill. One of these ended at a turntable which accessed Meledor (Grove) siding and which ran at a right angle to Melangoose Mill. The line that curves left dropped at 1 in 40 to Meledor Mill. (M.Dart)

GROVE

75. This southeasterly view shows Meledor (Grove) siding trailing in on the right on 31st May 1966. It was connected via a turntable to a siding at Melangoose Mill. The siding replaced a tramway. Much of the kiln is extant. (M Dart)

76. Wagons were winched along Grove siding, which rose on a gradient of 1 in 100. We look west, on 11th May 1968, at the capstan used for that purpose. (M.Dart)

VIRGINIA

77. We look north along the siding in the early 1920s. It extended well behind the camera, to serve another kiln where a connection had been made with a narrow gauge tramway from West Virginia kiln. Traffic for here was propelled from Melangoose Mill. (Imerys Minerals)

WEST TREVISCOE

78. As the branch continued it crossed the River Fal twice. On 31st May 1966 we look southeast at the siding, which formed a loop on the down side. An ungated works level crossing at Virginia followed shortly. (M.Dart)

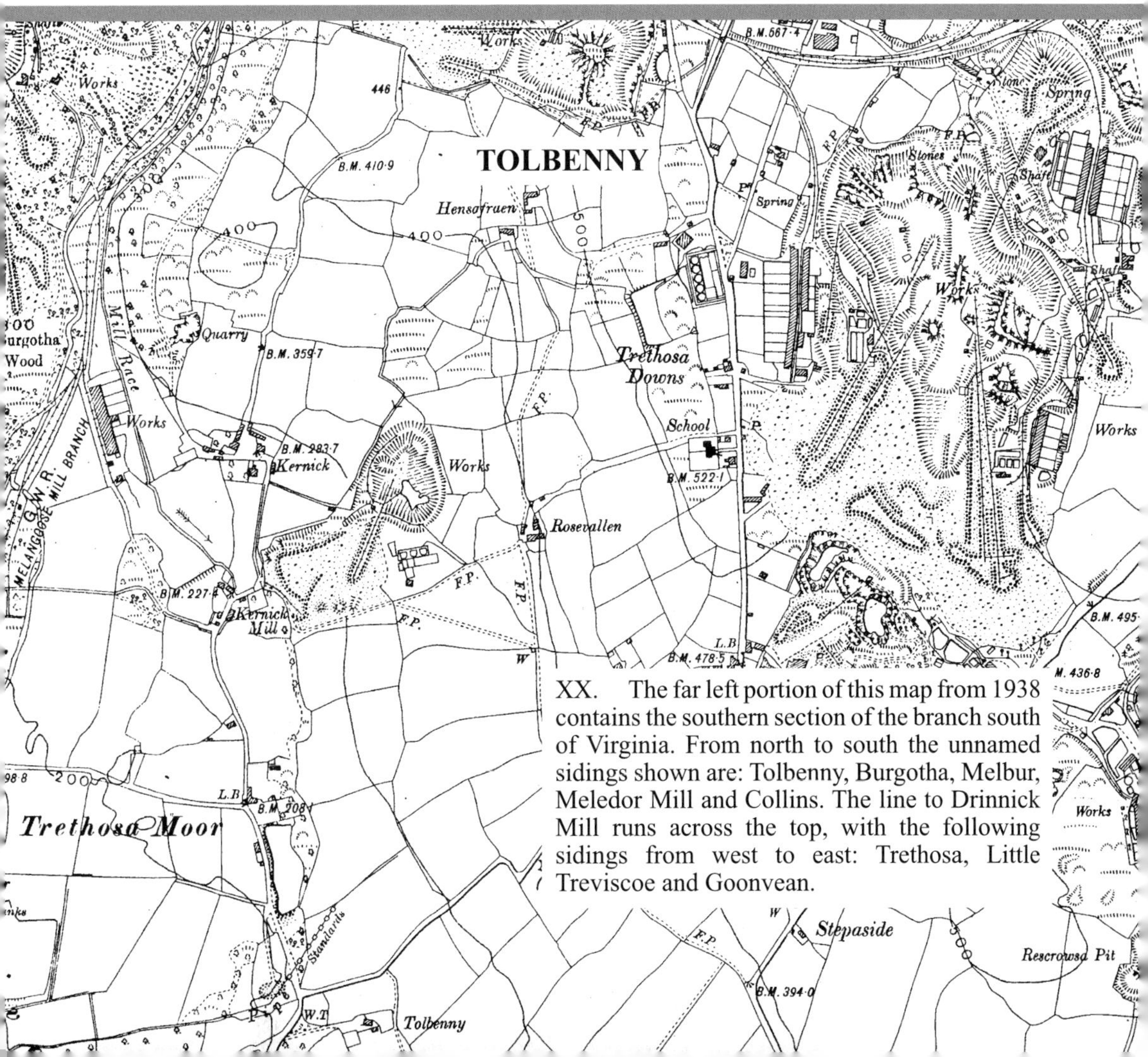

XX. The far left portion of this map from 1938 contains the southern section of the branch south of Virginia. From north to south the unnamed sidings shown are: Tolbenny, Burgotha, Melbur, Meledor Mill and Collins. The line to Drinnick Mill runs across the top, with the following sidings from west to east: Trethosa, Little Treviscoe and Goonvean.

79. A quarter of a mile further on, Tolbenny siding diverged on the down side; it was followed immediately on the up side by Burgotha siding. This siding was also called Lower Burgotha or Meledor Mill siding. We look south at the double junction on 14th June 1966. Meledor loops were on each side of the branch south of here. (M.Dart)

BURGOTHA

80. We look south west to Burgotha siding, which is seen on the right in this early 1920s view. It crossed the Fal to reach the kiln. (Imerys Minerals)

MELBUR

81. Seventeen chains beyond Burgotha siding, Melbur siding diverged on the up side; it is seen in this view from the early 1920s as we look southwest. This siding also crossed the Fal, and was the last to provide traffic on the branch. (Imerys Minerals)

MELEDOR MILL

82. We look north on 11th July 1955 as 0-6-0PT no.3635 shunts at the sidings. Tolbenny kiln is behind the wagons. (R.C.Riley/Transport Treasury)

83.   A scene at Meledor Mill looking south on 20th June 1958 features 2-6-2T no.5519 ready to depart with a short train. Empty open clay wagons stand by the loading wharf. (D.Lawrence/ H.Davies photos.)

84.   From Meledor Mill a siding continued over the fully gated Meledor level crossing, and followed the River Fal to reach New Meledor siding. This view looks south on 14th June 1966 and shows the crossing gates in the normal position which was closed across the track. (M.Dart)

NEW MELEDOR

85. New Meledor Clay Co siding was usually referred to as "Collins", as that was the captain's name. This view is southwest on 8th June 1968. The siding was the last but one source of traffic on the branch. (J.M.Tolson/F.Hornby)

> **Further photographs appear in *Branch Lines to Newquay*.**

BODINNICK/BODENNICK SIDING

This was on the up side of the main line approximately two thirds of a mile west of Burngullow. Sidings for the Bodennick Iron Ore Co. were authorised by the Cornwall Railways goods managers meeting on 29th September 1871. An eastward facing siding was laid to a loading wharf. From here the narrow gauge Sunny Corner Tramway ran to the iron mine. The siding closed at an unknown date but reopening was authorised on 2nd April 1880. Closure is believed to have occurred by September 1886 but the Cornwall Railway signal box survived in use as a gangers hut until about 1951 when it was demolished. Sadly no photographs of this location have been found. This reference is included to complete the information about facilities provided for mineral traffic.

8. NEWHAM BRANCH

This line was authorised by a West Cornwall Railway Act dated 3rd August 1846. It opened from Truro Road at Higher Town, Truro to Newham, for passengers and goods on 16th April 1855. The route crossed the Cornwall Railways line to Falmouth, on the level at Penwethers, until a trailing connection from the Falmouth line was opened on 23rd February 1894. Passenger services to Newham were withdrawn on 16th September 1863 following the opening of a connecting line from Truro Road to the Cornwall Railways station at Truro. The line remained open and handled considerable quantities of freight traffic. Complete closure took place on 7th November 1971. Earthworks were completed for a direct connecting line to the branch from immediately west of Higher Town Tunnel, but track was not laid.

1910

NEWHAM BRANCH.
SINGLE LINE.   GOODS TRAINS ONLY.

The Newham Branch is worked by Train Staff.   No Block Telegraph.
The Train Staff is a round one painted Black, lettered Penwithers Junction and Newham.
Only one Engine in steam must be allowed to be on this Branch at one and the same time.
The speed of Trains on this Branch must not exceed 20 miles per hour.

DOWN TRAINS.—WEEK DAYS ONLY.

Distance from Truro.		STATIONS.	K dep. A.M.	RR dep. P.M.	K dep. P.M.
M.	C.				
—	—	Truro .... dep.	10 12	12 20	4 5
—	52	Penwithers Jun. { arr.	10 15	12 24	4 7
		{ dep.	CS 10 20	CS 12 30	CS 4 11
3	3	Newham .... arr.	10 28	12 38	4 20

UP TRAINS.—WEEK DAYS ONLY.

STATIONS.	K dep. A.M.	RR dep. P.M.	K dep. P.M.
Newham .. .... dep.	11 45	1 8	5 15
Penwithers Jun. { arr.	11 55	1 16	5 23
{ dep.	CS 12 15	CS 1 21	CS 5 32
Truro .... arr.	12 18	1 25	5 35

1924

NEWHAM BRANCH.
SINGLE LINE.   GOODS TRAINS ONLY.   WEEK DAYS ONLY.

The Newham Branch is worked by Train Staff.   No Block Telegraph.
The Train Staff is a round one painted Black, lettered Penwithers Junction and Newham.
Only one Engine in Steam allowed on this Branch.
The speed of Trains on this Branch must not exceed 20 miles per hour.

Distance.		STATIONS.	Station No.	K dep. A.M.
M.	C.			
—	—	Truro .... dep.	2061	11 0
—	52	Penwithers { arr.	2070	11 3
		Jun. { dep.		11 13
		Stop Board		P
3	3	Newham .... arr.	2243	11 29

STATIONS.	K dep. P.M.
Newham .. .... dep.	12 40
Penwithers Jc. { arr.	12 50
{ dep.	12 55
Truro .... arr.	1 0

1951

TRURO AND NEWHAM.
SINGLE LINE, PENWITHERS JUNCTION TO NEWHAM WORKED BY TRAIN STAFF.
FREIGHT TRAINS ONLY.
Speed must not exceed 15 miles per hour.
One Engine in steam at a time, or two coupled.

Down Trains.   Week Days only.

M.P. Mileage.		Distance from Truro.		STATIONS.	Ruling Gradient 1 in	K SX a.m.	K SO a.m.	K SX p.m.
M.	C.	M.	C.					
300	63	—	—	TRURO .. dep	—	6 50	7 23	5 8
301	25	—	42	PENWITHERS JCT. { arr.	60 R.	6 55	7 28	5 13
				{ dep.	—	7 0	7 33	5 18
303	15	2	32	STOP BOARD	61 F.	P	P	P
303	65	3	3	NEWHAM arr.	52 F.	7 12	7 45	5 31

Up Trains.

STATIONS.	Ruling Gradient 1 in	K SX a.m.	K SO a.m.	K SX p.m.
NEWHAM dep.	—	8 0	8 48	6 25
PENWITHERS { arr.	52 R.	8 10	8 58	6 35
JCT. { dep.	—	8 17	9 8	6 40
TRURO arr.	60 F.	8 22	9 11	6 45

CALENICK

86. We look south east halfway along the line where it crossed the road from Truro to Falmouth near Calenick. The decking on the bridge is seen, along with the two different parapets in this undated view. The trackbed now forms a pleasant walk. (M.Dart coll.)

NEWHAM

87. We look northeast near the end of the branch, where a siding was opened on 3rd April 1955 to Truro gasworks. 2-6-2T no.5537 has brought empty coal wagons from it. These have been marshalled in to the train, which had been left on the branch, on 16th December 1961. The siding, which is hidden by the engine, was taken out of use on Christmas Day 1970. (L.Crosier)

88. A scene from 1958 looks south from the terminus at Newham. A 4500 class 2-6-2T shunts the sidings, which contain covered vans and empty coal wagons from Truro Gasworks, part of which is visible top right. (N.Simmons/H.Davies photos.)

Further photos appear in the *St.Austell to Penzance* and *Branch Lines to Falmouth, Helston and St.Ives* volumes.

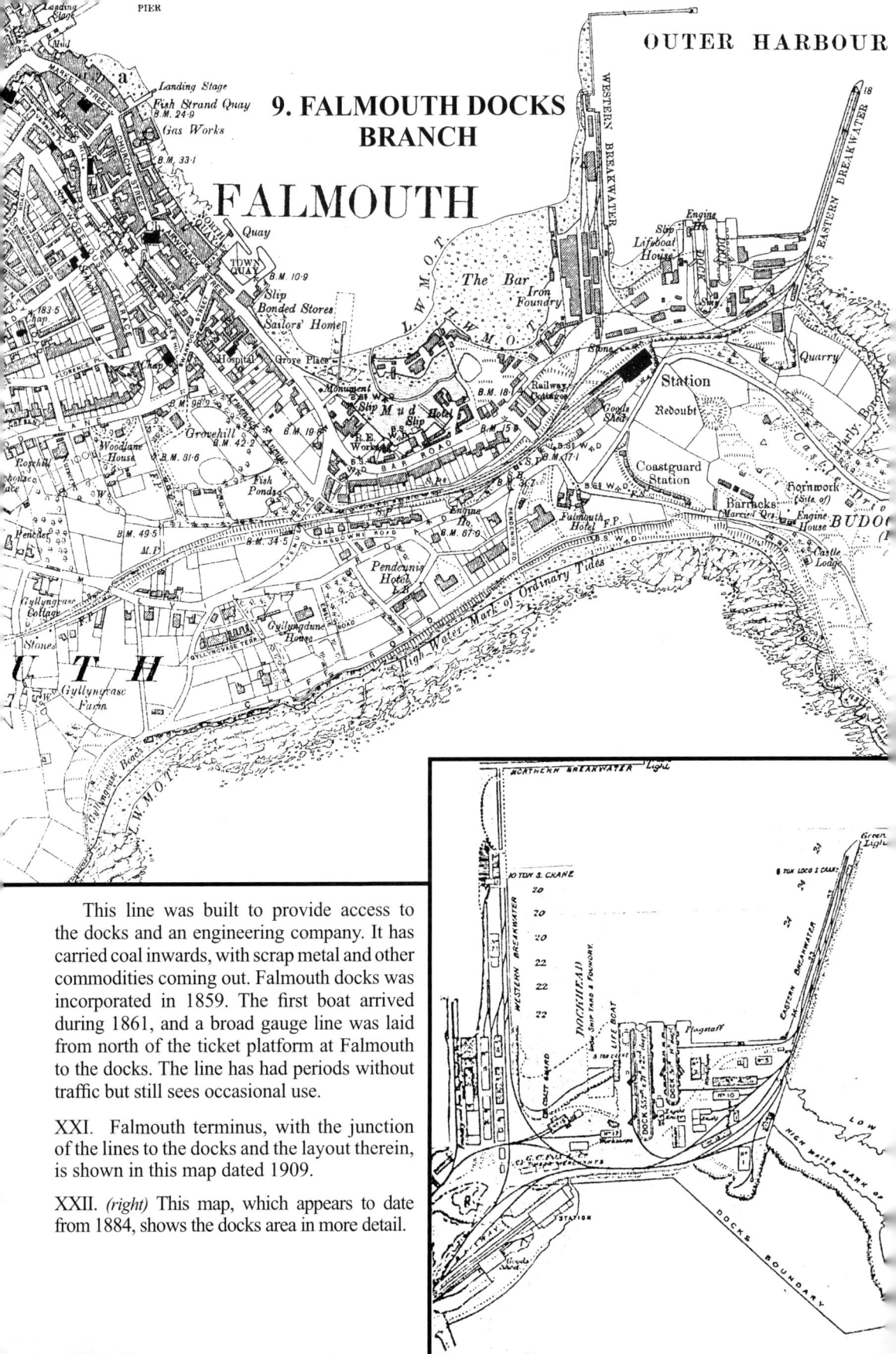

9. FALMOUTH DOCKS BRANCH

This line was built to provide access to the docks and an engineering company. It has carried coal inwards, with scrap metal and other commodities coming out. Falmouth docks was incorporated in 1859. The first boat arrived during 1861, and a broad gauge line was laid from north of the ticket platform at Falmouth to the docks. The line has had periods without traffic but still sees occasional use.

XXI. Falmouth terminus, with the junction of the lines to the docks and the layout therein, is shown in this map dated 1909.

XXII. *(right)* This map, which appears to date from 1884, shows the docks area in more detail.

89. The line to the docks left the Falmouth branch on the north side, just before the terminus, where there were exchange sidings. The line descended to the docks. We look southwest in the 1960s and see 0-4-0ST no.6, which was owned by the dock company, near the station. The locomotive was built by Peckett in 1919, works no.1530, and arrived at the docks from the Co-operative Wholesale Society at Irlam in October 1961. (M.Dart coll.)

90. Here we look northeast as Falmouth Docks 0-4-0ST no.6 shunts bitumen tank wagons in the exchange sidings near the passenger terminus in the 1960s. (M.Dart coll.)

91. A rare photo shows one of the 0-4-0 vertical boilered locomotives in broad gauge days, before 1892, in the docks outside one of the sheds. These locomotives were built locally by Sara & Burgess of Penryn and were converted to operate on standard gauge track. (M.Dart coll.)

92. We are inside the engine shed at the docks on 17th April 1963. A pair of 0-4-0STs are present. At the rear is no.3 (Hawthorn Leslie no.3597 built in 1926). The front resident is no.6- Peckett no.1530 built in 1919. No.3 is preserved on the Plym Valley Railway and no.6 is at Poldark Mine, Wendron near Helston. (M.Dart)

93. A scene in the docks on 17th April 1963 shows 0-4-0ST no.4 (Hawthorn Leslie no.3670 of 1927) moving around the system to reach the loco shed. (M.Dart)

Further scenes appear in *Branch Lines to Falmouth, Helston and St.Ives.*

94. For several periods the connecting lines to the docks lay moribund. They were brought back into use to convey coal to a local delivery merchant who used the docks as a transfer area. No.37674 remained on the connecting line, with wagons, over a weekend. It is featured in this easterly facing view near the entrance gates to the docks on 14th July 1997. (M.Dart)

10. TRESEVEAN BRANCH

This line connected tin, copper and arsenic mines to the main line. It facilitated the transport of ore to ports and the delivery of supplies to the mines. The line was authorised by the Hayle Railway Act dated 27th June 1834 and opened on 23rd June 1838. An Act dated 3rd August 1846 empowered the West Cornwall Railway to purchase the HR and to rebuild it with diversions in places. It was also to extend in each direction to form a continuous route from Truro to Penzance. The WCR took possession of the HR on 3rd November 1846 and closed it for rebuilding on 16th February 1852. The new route and lines were opened on 11th March 1852. From 1st July 1865, the WCR was leased jointly by the GWR, the Bristol & Exeter Railway and the South Devon Railway. The HR was transferred to the three companies absolutely on 1st January 1866.

The B&E and the SDR amalgamated with the GWR, and the WCR thus became part of the GWR 1st August 1878. The 1865 Act provided for the dissolution of the WCR, but due to a mistake, it was not wound up and continued to nominally exist until the Transport Act of 1947 transferred it to the British Transport Commission. The Tresevean branch closed on 1st January 1936.

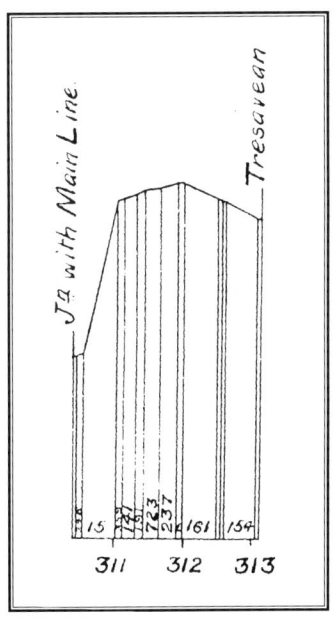

22nd September 1924

XXIII. This 1909 map shows Redruth Junction (left). The original Hayle Railway diverges northeast to its Redruth terminus, which later became the goods station. The Tresevean line runs southeast. The straight section is the incline which commenced slightly to the north of the overline bridge and ended near Wheal Uny. The 4ft gauge Redruth & Chasewater Railway is shown on the right of the map.

TRESEVEAN INCLINE

95.   This view from 1934 looks southeast from Redruth Junction. and shows the foot of the half-mile long incline, which was graded at 1 in 15. A locomotive placed up to four wagons on the down line at the foot. It ran light to the top on the up line and picked up loaded wagons and then descended with these whilst attached to a continuous cable which simultaneously hauled the four empty wagons up. The cable is visible on the up line. (J.O.Mulhaus)

96.   We look south east, up the incline from the overline bridge shown in the previous picture, on 10th June 1933. Rollers are visible on both lines and the cable is on the down line. A footpath crossed the incline near the summit, adjacent to the distant buildings. (M.Dart coll.)

97. The shell of the incline operators hut lingered on at the summit. It is shown as we look north on 17th June 1958. (D.Lawrence/H.Davies photos.)

LANNER HILL

98. Horses worked trains over the remainder of the branch from the top of the incline. After two thirds of a mile the line crossed the track of the four-foot gauge Redruth & Chasewater Railway on the level. The R&C passed in front of the yard gate that we see on 4th March 1937. We look southeast to the storage yards, which were provided by each company for the exchange of coal and ore. A siding diverged to the right to serve this storage yard, which was near the top of Lanner Hill. The location was called Wheal Beauchamp or Bassett Yard. (M.Dart coll.)

99. We look south a short distance beyond Wheal Beauchamp on 10th June 1933 where a rough track crossed the line. The old clerestory coach appears to be inhabited, as it has curtains at the windows. (M.Dart coll.)

TRESEVEAN MINE

XXIV. On a map from 1906 the branch comes in from the north, heads south and turns east to reach its terminus at Tresevean Mine.

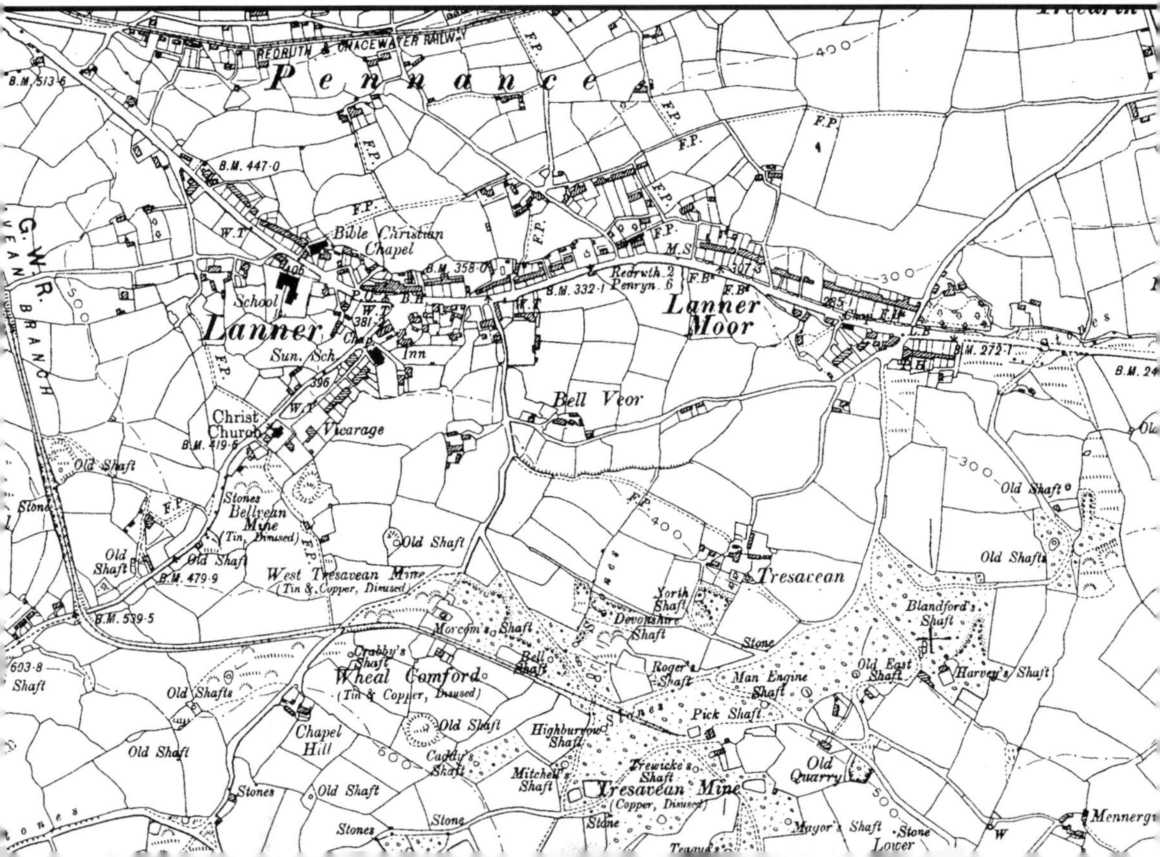

100. A view southeast in 1934, includes the end of the line at Tresevean Mine 2½ miles from Redruth Junction. The mine engine house, and a loop that was provided for shunting are featured. (J.O.Mulhaus)

11. PORTREATH BRANCH

This line was laid to transport ore to the harbour and to bring coal, wood and other supplies back to the mines. It was one of the HRs branch lines which opened on 23rd December 1837. The line closed beyond North Pool on 1st January 1936 and the remaining portion followed on 1st April 1938.

June 1879

```
PORTREATH  BRANCH.—GOODS.
              DOWN TRAINS.
                                          A.M.      P.M.
  Carn Brea Yard  ...  ...  ...  ...  departure  10 30   5 30
  Portreath        ...  ...  ...  ...  arrival    10 45   5 45

              UP TRAINS.
                                          A.M.      P.M.
  Portreath   ...  ...  ...  ...  ..  departure  11  0    6  0
  Carn Brea Yard  ...  ...  ...  ...  arrival    11 15    6 15
```

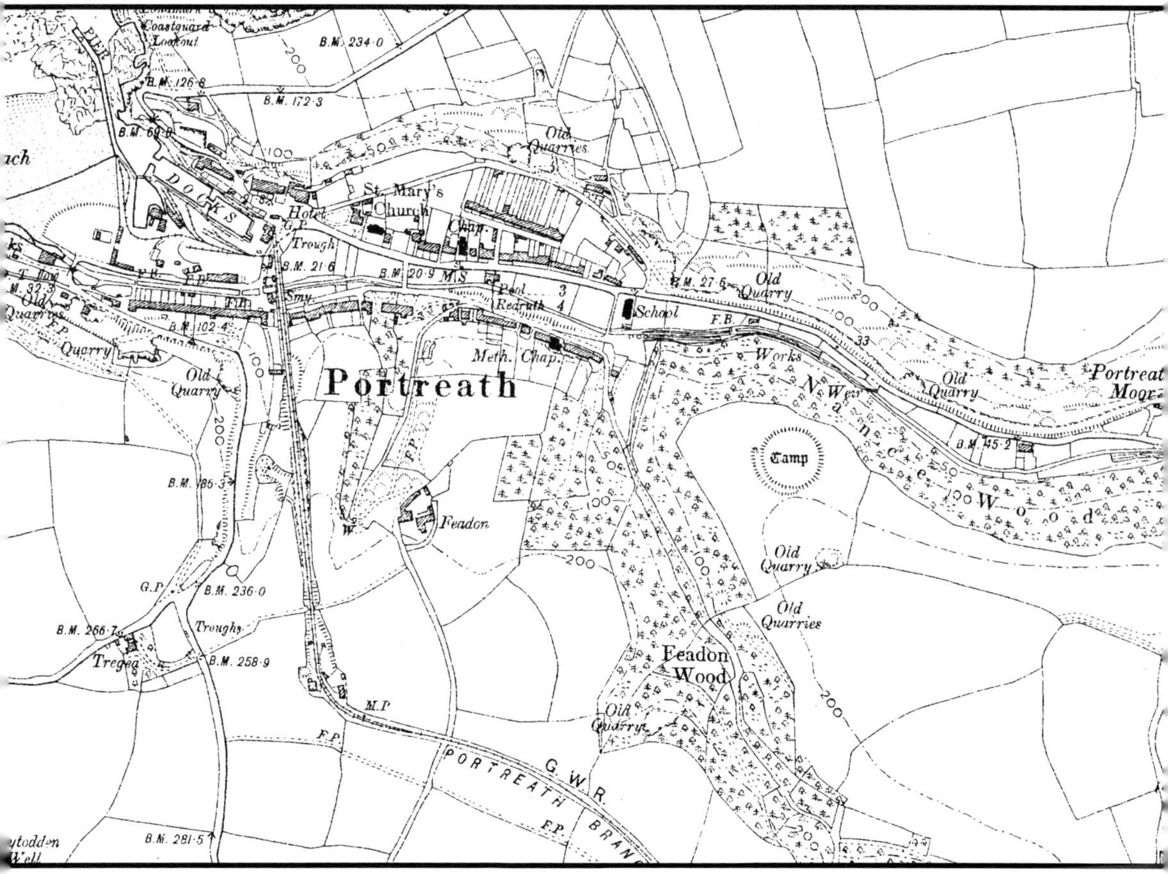

XXV. A 1906 map shows the incline as the long straight section heading south from the docks. The Poldice Tramway of 1809 ran east from the docks.

September 1924

PORTREATH BRANCH.
Worked by Train Staff.   No Block Telegraph.
SINGLE LINE.   GOODS TRAINS ONLY.
Only one Engine in Steam must be allowed to be on this Branch at one and the same time.

from Carn Brea Yard.	M. C.	DOWN TRAINS—WEEK DAYS ONLY.					UP TRAINS.—WEEK DAYS ONLY.			
		STATIONS.	Station No.	1 K arr.	1 K dep.		STATIONS.	Station No.	1 K arr.	1 K dep.
				A.M.	P.M.				P.M.	P.M.
—	—	Carn Brea Yard	2078	11 54	12 20	Works Sidings only T.TH. and S.O. and runs to Portreath on Thurs. only.	Portreath		1 0	1 20
—	—	Illogan Highway Crossing	2272	—	—		Fair Field Crossing		..	..
0 35		Illogan Highway or Wheal Agar Sdng.	2273	T. TH. S.O.			Lovely Cottage Crossing		..	..
0 61		North Pool Siding	2274	—	—		Illogan Gate Crossing		T. TH. S.O.	
—	—	Illogan Gate Crsng.	2275	—	—		North Pool Siding		—	—
—	—	Lovely Cottage Crsg.	2276	—	—		Illogan Highway or Wheal Agar Siding		—	—
—	—	Fair Field Crossing	2277	—	—		Illogan Highway Crossing		—	—
3 6		Portreath	2278	1 0	1 20		Carn Brea Yard		2 5	..

NOTE.—The Illogan, Lovely Cottage, and Fairfield Level Crossing Gates are worked by the Guard, and the key is kept in the Signal Box at Carn Brea Yard. Before proceeding on to the Portreath Branch, the Guard must apply to the Signalman for the key, and hand it to him on his return. The Gates must be kept across the Railway when NOT in use, and the Guard must, before leaving Carn Brea Yard, satisfy himself that the Driver understands the arrangement.

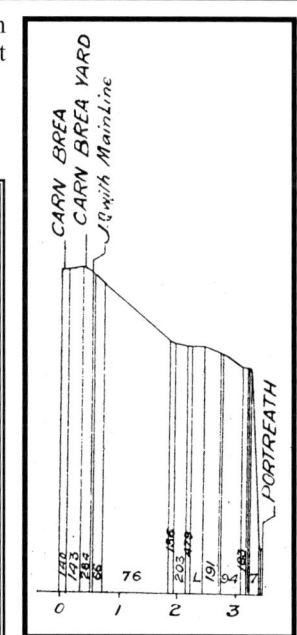

PORTREATH JUNCTION

101. We look north in 1934 at Portreath Junction, which was immediately east of Carn Brea yard. The branch to Portreath diverged from the main line to the left of the water tank. The line diverging to the right from the branch was a ballast siding which was brought into use during 1910. (J.O.Mulhaus)

ILLOGAN HIGHWAY

102. A quarter of a mile from the junction, the line passed over the old main road from Redruth to Camborne at Illogan Highway level crossing, which is shown in this north facing aspect in March 1937. The crossing keepers hut is prominent. Illogan Highway (Wheal Agar) siding, which formed a loop, followed on the up side a few yards along the branch. After a further half mile was North Pool siding, which also was a loop was on the down side. Within the next mile two minor tracks crossed the line. These were followed by Lovely Cottage level crossing. (M.Dart.coll.)

FAIRFIELD

103. The next gated level crossing was at Fairfield, near Painters Lane End, where the line crossed a minor road. We look north west, on 24th April 1937, to the crossing keepers hut. (R.S.Carpenter photos.)

PORTREATH INCLINE

104. This interesting view is dated 24th April 1937. We look northeast and see on the left the engine house for the incline winder. On the right is a small building for the incline look-out man. The single line became double before descending the incline. The short-lived Fairfield timber siding was a short distance, behind the camera, on the down side. (R.S.Carpenter photos.)

105. We look south up the incline in the early 1900s; it was about ¼ mile in length and was graded at 1 in 7. Rollers are between the rails, with winding cable on the down line. Twin turntables gave access to a network of sidings that served the south side of the dock. (M.Dart coll.)

PORTREATH HARBOUR

XXVI. This section of a 25ins to 1 mile map from 1879 shows the layout of lines from the bottom of the incline to and around the harbour.

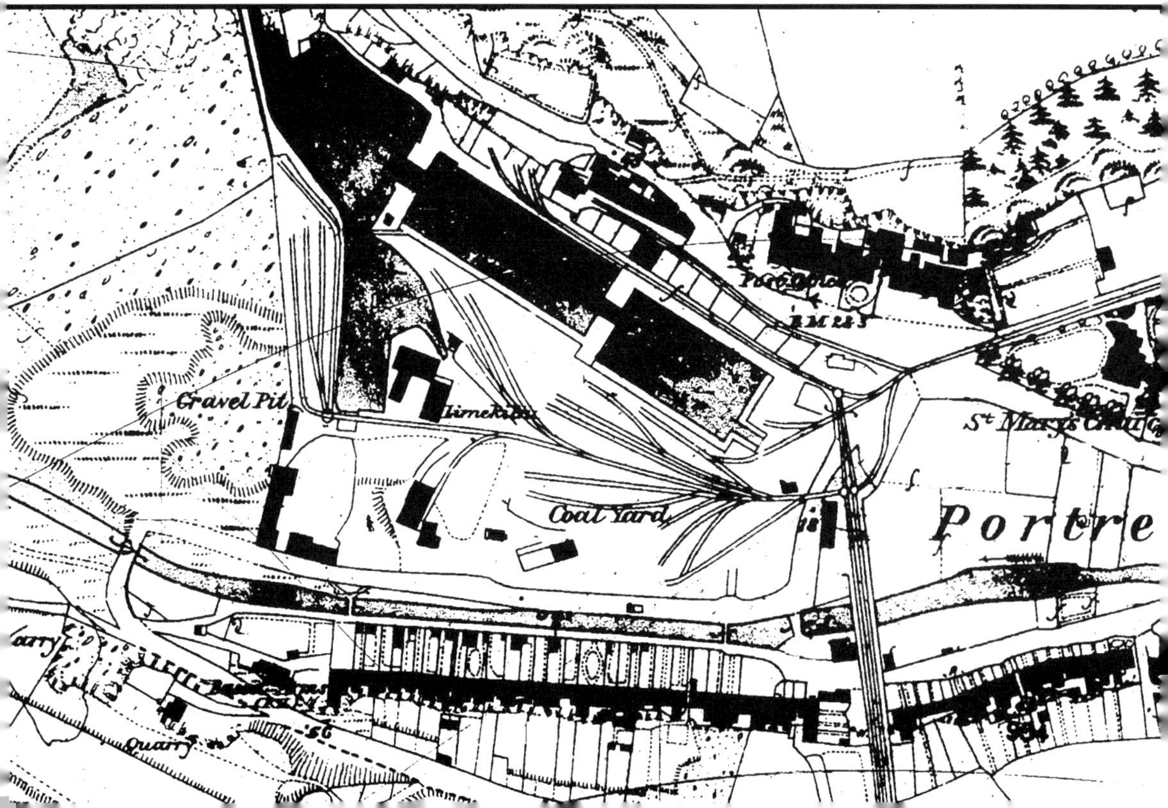

106. Here we are on the south side of the dock on 24th April 1937, looking west. A lime kiln can be seen on the left, with piles of coal on the right and a steam shovel is partly in the view. (R.S.Carpenter)

107. We look south east at a panorama of the harbour in the 1920s. A coaster is in the inner dock, with two more in the outer dock. Coal is being off-loaded using a steam shovel. Wagons loaded with coal await passage up the incline. One wagon was raised per journey. The incline is visible upper left. Horses were used to shunt at the harbour. This area has changed beyond all recognition, being occupied by housing development. (R.Winnen coll.)

CARN BREA

108. GWR 0-6-0ST no.1799 is standing in the yard outside Carn Brea engine shed in about 1905. It regularly worked on the lines to Portreath and Tresevean. (M.Dart.coll.)

12. NORTH CROFTY BRANCH

This short line, which served tin and copper mines, was another of the HRs branches with opening taking place on 23rd December 1837. The line closed beyond Tuckingmill early in 1937. The remaining portion of the line closed on 1st December 1948.

NORTH CROFTY BRANCH.
SINGLE LINE. GOODS TRAINS ONLY. Worked by Train Staff. No Block Telegraph.

Distance from N. Crofty Junction.	STATIONS.	arr.	dep.	STATIONS.	arr.	dep.
M. C.			K		K	
0 0	North Crofty Junction	20d1	C R	North Crofty Siding	C R	
0 15	Cook's Kitchen Siding	2252	C R	Tuckingmill Siding	C R	
0 37	Tuckingmill Siding	2263	C R	Cook's Kitchen Siding	C R	
0 43	North Crofty Siding	2291	—	North Crofty Junction	—	

There are several unprotected Accommodation Crossings on this Branch. Guards are responsible for seeing that the Crossings are clear before allowing Trains to pass over them.

109. Views of this line were very difficult to locate. This interesting scene looks west in about 1910. We see the 2ft gauge horse-worked tramway that ran from Robinsons shaft to South Crofty mine. It crossed the North Crofty branch and passed the old Cornish stamps engine house to reach the new electrically driven Californian stamps. These were in the lower building at the rear and were installed in 1908. (J.O.Mulhaus)

110. This southward facing vista from 1924 shows the branch terminating by the old main road from Redruth to Camborne at Tuckingmill. Empty wagons are on a siding that served a coal depot. The stamps complex is top right. A tramway crossed the line and Dudnance Lane and ran east to Robinsons shaft. The complex of Cooks Kitchen mine is top centre with the Climax Rock Drill Works just above the main road. Below the main road is the depot of the 3ft 6in gauge electrically worked Camborne & Redruth Tramway. A mineral branch line from this headed west, crossed the road and turned north towards Tolvaddon stamps. The round pit at the bottom right is the disused shaft of North Crofty Mine which was served by a continuation of the line across the main road. The shaft was abandoned in 1911 and the track was removed. (J.O.Mulhaus)

13. ROSKEAR BRANCH

This line was yet another branch of the HR, which opened on 23rd December 1837. It served tin and copper mines and an engineering works and ran through the eastern suburbs of Camborne. Closure beyond Holmans no.3 works occurred on an unspecified date in 1963. The remainder of the line closed on 31st January 1981.

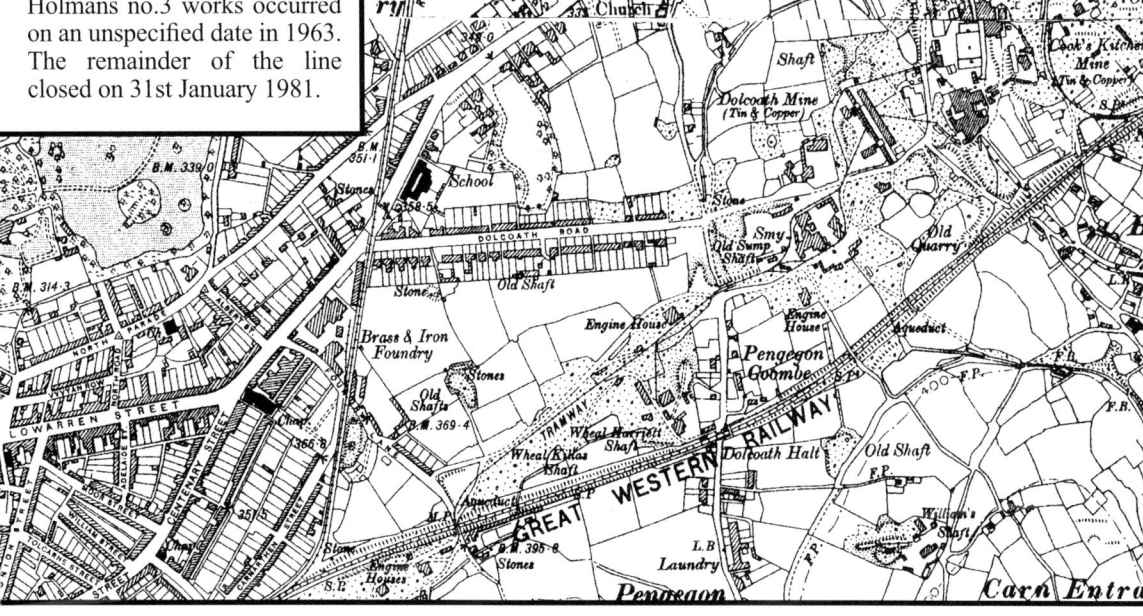

XXVII. A survey from 1908 shows the Roskear and North Crofty branches diverging north from their respective junctions. Several mine tramways are shown.

111. This short branch was not visited by many photographers. This photo was taken in 1924 looking east from Roskear Road level crossing which was just below the centre of the picture. The track continued north to Holmans New Cornwall boiler works at North Roskear. The sidings by the crossing served Holmans no.3 foundry. The North Crofty branch can be seen at the top of the picture as it headed south. (J.O.Mulhaus)

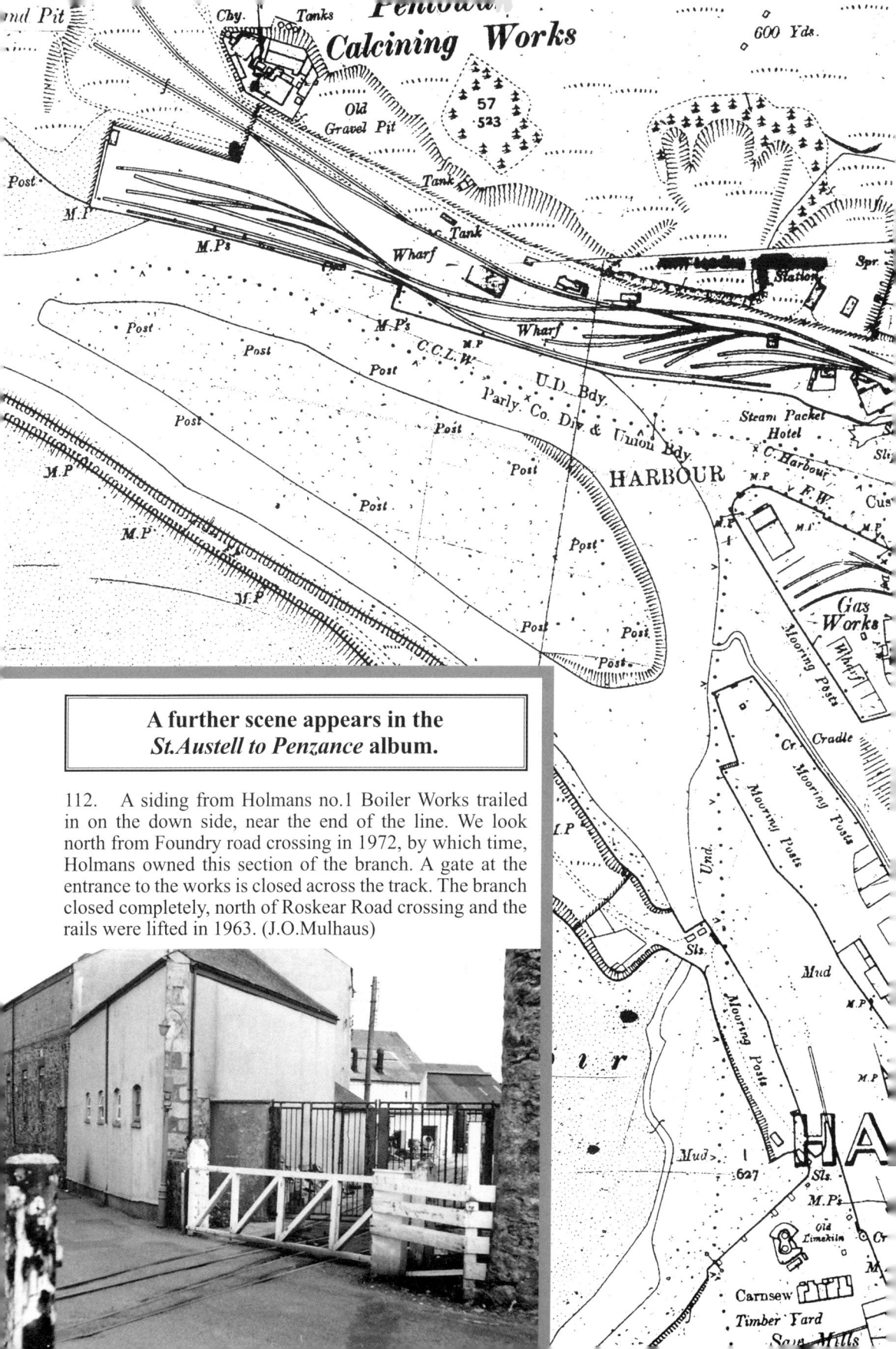

A further scene appears in the St.Austell to Penzance album.

112.   A siding from Holmans no.1 Boiler Works trailed in on the down side, near the end of the line. We look north from Foundry road crossing in 1972, by which time, Holmans owned this section of the branch. A gate at the entrance to the works is closed across the track. The branch closed completely, north of Roskear Road crossing and the rails were lifted in 1963. (J.O.Mulhaus)

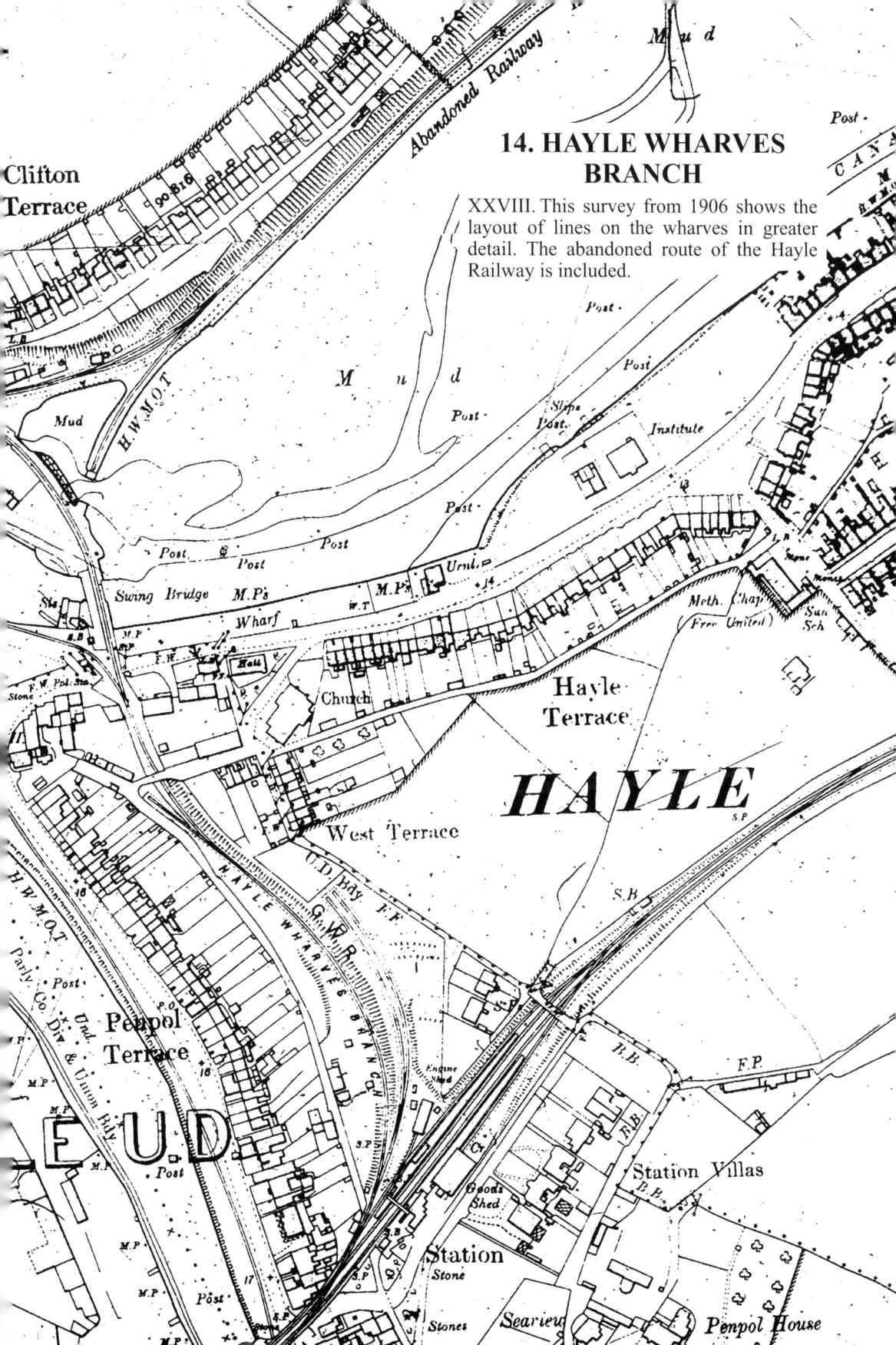

14. HAYLE WHARVES BRANCH

XXVIII. This survey from 1906 shows the layout of lines on the wharves in greater detail. The abandoned route of the Hayle Railway is included.

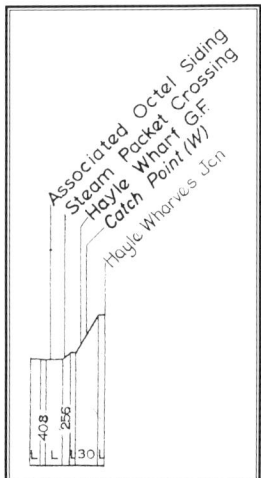

The HR opened the original line to the wharves at Hayle, as stated earlier. From Redruth it ran via a viaduct at Penponds and descended inclines at Penponds and at Angarrick. It continued near the river, which it crossed to reach the wharves. The WCR completely re-routed this section of line to avoid the inclines and constructed a new line to the wharves from a new station at Hayle. This line descended on a gradient of 1 in 30 and closed on 31st January 1981.

Since the mid 1800s an explosives works had existed in the sand dunes northeast of Hayle, to supply the mines in the area. On the southwest side of it, 1½ miles of the original HR line had been retained to access sand pits. A private line of 2¼ miles was constructed from this old line in 1917. It was laid partly on the former HR trackbed and serviced the greatly expanded works of the National Explosive Company which was a subsidiary of Nobels Explosive Co. The line closed during 1919.

HAYLE AND HAYLE WHARVES.

The speed on this Branch not to exceed 10 miles per hour.

SINGLE LINE. FREIGHT TRAINS ONLY. WORKED BY TELEPHONE AND TRAIN STAFF.

Only one Engine in Steam or two or more coupled must be allowed to be on this Branch at one and the same time.

Mileage	Down Trains. STATIONS		Ruling Gradient 1 in	Week Days only. a.m.	a.m.	Up Trains. STATIONS		Ruling Gradient 1 in	a.m.	p.m.
M. C.										
— —	HAYLE	dep.	—	10 0	11 50	HAYLE WHARVES	dep.	30 R	11 15	12 20
— 54	HAYLE WHARVES	arr.	30 F	10 5	11 55	HAYLE	arr.	—	11 20	12 25

113. Looking north in June 1958 we see, from left to right, the line to the wharves dropping at 1 in 30, the small yard alongside the station, the disused engine shed, the up loop and Hayle passenger station with the signal box on the up platform. (N.Simmons/H.Davies photos.)

September 1951

114. A train is almost at the top of the incline from Hayle wharves on 14th June 1956. It is hauled by 2-6-2T no.4540 and was photographed from the station platform. The yard contained several wagons and possessed a crane of 15 ton capacity. (R.Cogger/(M.Dart coll.)

115. We look northeast to the original HR terminus station on 10th June 1933. It was situated below and just to the north of the viaduct. (M.Dart coll.)

116. Looking north on 14th June 1956, 2-6-2T no.4540 is on the swing bridge with a short train. It is waiting for the signalman to open the gates over the old main road. The line branching left led to Harvey's Penpol siding. (M.Dart coll.)

117. We look along the power station coal wharf on the northeast side of the complex in the 1920s. Two steam shovels are unloading coal from the coaster ESKWOOD and a gantry shovel is unloading wagons of coal near the hopper. It fed a continuous belt that ran in a trough to the power station. (R Winnen coll.)

118. A train on the northeast side of the wharves waits on 26th July 1979 to depart with tank wagons from the Esso siding. It is hauled by 1250hp Sulzer diesel electric no.25057. (D.H.Mitchell.)

Further views appear in *St.Austell to Penzance.*

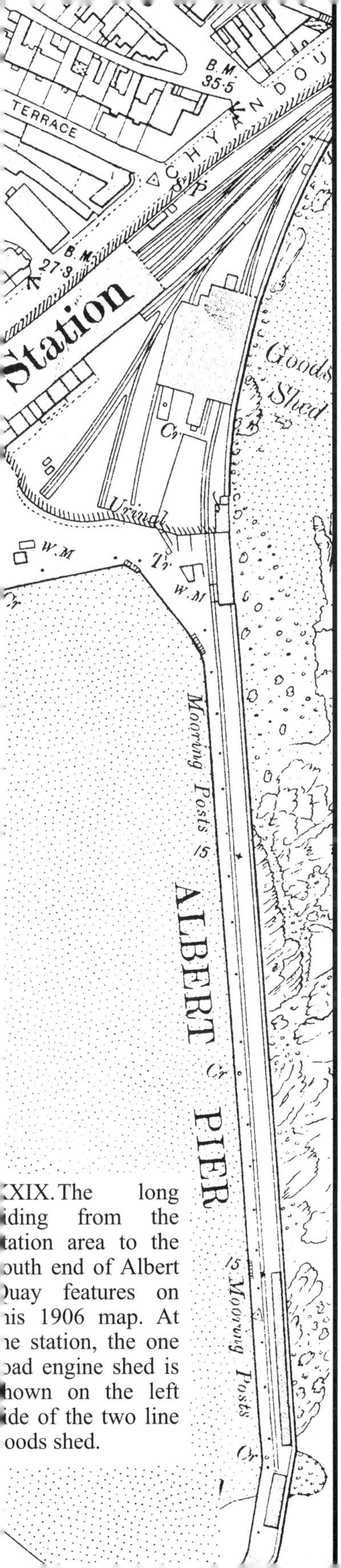

15. ALBERT QUAY SIDING, PENZANCE

This line appears to have opened by an agreement with Penzance Town Council dated 29th April 1869, but closed at an unknown date after 1938 and was lifted. It was reinstated on 4th August 1949 by an agreement with Western Salvaging Company, which became Penzance Shippers and Salvage from 11th July 1957. The line was taken out of use during 1960 and was supposedly removed during September 1967. Some rails remained in place in 2004.

119. This panorama of Penzance from 1937 looks south and shows the long siding which contains vans and wagons. It ran to the end of Albert Quay, which is to left of centre in the picture. The line ran through the goods shed to reach the quay. The original single road engine shed stood between the goods shed and the passenger station. (T.Corin/M.Dart coll.)

Further photos are included in the *St.Austell to Penzance* album.

120. The concluding view in this album looks north along the remaining disused track on the quay. Despite closure in 1960 most of the rails remained, albeit buried in places. We see the re-roofed passenger station in the centre of the picture on 7th April 2002. (M.Dart)

XIX. The long siding from the station area to the south end of Albert Quay features on this 1906 map. At the station, the one road engine shed is shown on the left side of the two line goods shed.

**Easebourne Lane, Midhurst
West Sussex. GU29 9AZ**

A-0 906520 B-1 873793 C-1 901706 D-1 904474

OOP Out of Print at time of printing - Please check current availability **BROCHURE AVAILABLE SHOWING NEW TITLES**
Tel:01730 813169   www.middletonpress.co.uk   email:info@middletonpress.co.uk

A
Abergavenny to Merthyr C 91 5
Aldgate & Stepney Tramways B 70 7
Allhallows - Branch Line to A 62 2
Alton - Branch Lines to A 11 8
Andover to Southampton A 82 7
Ascot - Branch Lines around A 64 9
Ashburton - Branch Line to A 95 2
Ashford - Steam to Eurostar B 67 7
Ashford to Dover A 48 7
Austrian Narrow Gauge D 04 7
Avonmouth - BL around D 42 X
B
Banbury to Birmingham D 27 6
Barking to Southend C 80 X
Barnet & Finchley Tramways B 93 6
Barry - BL around D 50 0
Basingstoke to Salisbury A 89 4
Bath Green Park to Bristol C 36 2
Bath to Evercreech Junction A 60 6
Bath Tramways B 86 3
Battle over Portsmouth 1940 A 29 0
Battle over Sussex 1940 A 79 7
Bedford to Wellingborough D 31 4
Betwixt Petersfield & Midhurst A 94 0
Blitz over Sussex 1941-42 B 35 9
Bodmin - Branch Lines around B 83 9
Bognor at War 1939-45 B 59 6
Bombers over Sussex 1943-45 B 51 0
Bournemouth & Poole Trys B 47 2 OOP
Bournemouth to Evercreech Jn A 46 0
Bournemouth to Weymouth A 57 6
Bournemouth Trolleybuses C 10 9
Bradford Trolleybuses D 19 5
Brecon to Neath D 43 8
Brecon to Newport D 16 0
Brickmaking in Sussex B 19 7
Brightons Tramways B 02 2
Brighton to Eastbourne A 16 9
Brighton to Worthing A 03 7
Bristols Tramways B 57 X
Bristol to Taunton D 03 9
Bromley South to Rochester B 23 5 OOP
Bude - Branch Line to B 29 4
Burnham to Evercreech Jn A 68 1
Burton & Ashby Tramways C 51 6
C
Camberwell & West Norwood Tys B 22 7
Canterbury - Branch Lines around B 58 8
Caterham & Tattenham Corner B 25 1
Changing Midhurst C 15 X
Chard and Yeovil - BLs around C 30 3
Charing Cross to Dartford A 75 4
Charing Cross to Orpington A 96 7
Cheddar - Branch Line to B 90 1
Cheltenham to Andover C 43 5
Chesterfield Tramways D 37 3
Chesterfield Trolleybuses D 51 9
Chichester to Portsmouth A 14 2 OOP
Clapham & Streatham Tramways B 97 9
Clapham Junction - 50 yrs C 06 0
Clapham Junction to Beckenham Jn B 36 7
Clevedon & Portishead - BLs to D 18 7
Collectors Trains, Trolleys & Trams B 29 2
Cornish Narrow Gauge D 56 X
Crawley to Littlehampton A 34 7
Cromer - Branch Lines around C 26 5
Croydons Tramways B 42 1
Croydons Trolleybuses B 73 1 OOP
Croydon to East Grinstead B 48 0
Crystal Palace (HL) & Catford Loop A 87 8
D
Darlington Trolleybuses D 33 0
Dartford to Sittingbourne B 34 0
Derby Tramways D 17 9
Derby Trolleybuses C 72 9
Derwent Valley - Branch Line to the D 06 3
Didcot to Banbury D 02 0
Didcot to Swindon C 84 2
Didcot to Winchester C 13 3
Douglas to Peel C 88 5
Douglas to Port Erin C 55 9
Douglas to Ramsey D 39 X
Dover's Tramways B 24 3
Dover to Ramsgate A 78 9
E
Ealing to Slough C 42 7
Eastbourne to Hastings A 27 4

East Cornwall Mineral Railways D 22 5
East Croydon to Three Bridges A 53 3
East Grinstead - Branch Lines to A 07 X
East Ham & West Ham Tramways B 52 9
East Kent Light Railway A 61 4
East London - Branch Lines of C 44 3
East London Line B 80 4
East Ridings Secret Resistance D 21 7
Edgware & Willesden Tramways C 18 4
Effingham Junction - BLs around A 74 6
Eltham & Woolwich Tramways B 74 X
Ely to Cambridge D 55 1 - PUB APRIL
Ely to Kings Lynn C 53 2
Ely to Norwich C 90 7
Embankment & Waterloo Tramways B 41 3
Enfield & Wood Green Trys C 03 6 OOP
Enfield Town & Palace Gates - BL to D 32 2
Epsom to Horsham A 30 4
Euston to Harrow & Wealdstone C 89 3
Exeter & Taunton Tramways B 32 4
Exeter to Barnstaple B 15 4
Exeter to Newton Abbot C 49 4
Exeter to Tavistock B 69 3
Exmouth - Branch Lines to B 00 6 OOP
F
Fairford - Branch Line to A 52 5
Falmouth, Helston & St. Ives - BL to C 74 5
Fareham to Salisbury A 67 3
Faversham to Dover B 05 7 OOP
Felixstowe & Aldeburgh - BL to D 20 9
Fenchurch Street to Barking C 20 6
Festiniog - 50 yrs of enterprise C 83 4
Festiniog in the Fifties B 68 5
Festiniog in the Sixties B 91 X
Finsbury Park to Alexandra Palace C 02 8
Frome to Bristol B 77 4
Fulwell - Trams, Trolleys & Buses D 11 X
G
Garraway Father & Son A 20 7 OOP
Gloucester to Bristol D 35 7
Gosport & Horndean Trys B 92 8 OOP
Gosport - Branch Lines around A 36 3
Great Yarmouth Tramways D 13 6
Greenwich & Dartford Tramways B 14 6 OOP
Guildford to Redhill A 63 0
H
Hammersmith & Hounslow Trys C 33 8
Hampshire Narrow Gauge D 36 5
Hampshire Waterways A 84 3 OOP
Hampstead & Highgate Tramways B 53 7
Harrow to Watford D 14 4
Hastings to Ashford A 37 1 OOP
Hastings Tramways B 18 9
Hastings Trolleybuses B 81 2 OOP
Hawkhurst - Branch Line A 66 5
Hayling - Branch Line to A 12 6
Haywards Heath to Seaford A 28 2 OOP
Henley, Windsor & Marlow - BL to C77 X
Hereford to Newport D 74 3
Hitchin to Peterborough D 07 1
Holborn & Finsbury Tramways B 79 0
Holborn Viaduct to Lewisham A 81 9
Horsham - Branch Lines to A 02 9
Huddersfield Trolleybuses C 92 3
Hull Trolleybuses D 24 1
Huntingdon - Branch Lines around A 93 2
I
Ilford & Barking Tramways B 61 8
Ilford to Shenfield C 97 4
Ilfracombe - Branch Line to B 21 9
Ilkeston & Glossop Tramways D 40 3
Industrial Rlys of the South East A 09 6
Ipswich to Saxmundham C 41 9 OOP
Isle of Wight Lines - 50 yrs C 12 5
K
Kent & East Sussex Waterways A 72 X
Kent Narrow Gauge C 45 1
Kingsbridge - Branch Line to C 98 2
Kingston & Hounslow Loops A 83 5
Kingston & Wimbledon Tramways B 56 1
Kingswear - Branch Line to C 17 6
L
Lambourn - Branch Line to C 70 2
Launceston & Princetown - BL to C 19 2
Lewisham & Catford Tramways B 26 X
Lewisham to Dartford A 92 4
Lines around Wimbledon B 75 8
Liverpool Street to Chingford D 01 2

Liverpool Street to Ilford C 34 6
Liverpool Tramways - Eastern C 04 4
Liverpool Tramways - Northern C 46 X
Liverpool Tramways - Southern C 23 0
London Bridge to Addiscombe B 20 0 OOP
London Bridge to East Croydon A 58 4
London Chatham & Dover Railway A 88 6
London Termini - Past and Proposed D 00 4
London to Portsmouth Waterways B 43 X
Longmoor - Branch Lines to A 41 X
Looe - Branch Line to C 22 2
Lyme Regis - Branch Line to A 45 2
Lynton - Branch Line to B 04 9
M
Maidstone & Chatham Tramways B 40 5
Maidstone Trolleybuses C 00 1 OOP
March - Branch Lines around B 09 X
Margate & Ramsgate Tramways C 52 4
Marylebone to Rickmansworth D49 7
Midhurst - Branch Lines around A 49 5
Midhurst - Branch Lines to A 01 0 OOP
Military Defence of West Sussex A 23 1
Military Signals, South Coast C 54 0
Minehead - Branch Line to A 80 0
Mitcham Junction Lines B 01 4
Mitchell & company C 59 1
Moreton-in-Marsh to Worcester D 26 8
Moretonhampstead - Branch Line to C 27 3
N
Newbury to Westbury C 66 4
Newport - Branch Lines to A 26 6
Newquay - Branch Lines to C 71 0
Newton Abbot to Plymouth C 60 5
Northern France Narrow Gauge C 75 3
North East German Narrow Gauge D 44 6
North Kent Tramways B 44 8
North London Line B 94 4
North Woolwich - BLs around C 65 6
Norwich Tramways C 40 0
Notts & Derby Tramway D 53 5
O
Orpington to Tonbridge B 03 0
Oxford to Moreton-in-Marsh D 15 2
P
Paddington to Ealing C 37 0
Paddington to Princes Risborough C 81 8
Padstow - Branch Line to B 54 5
Plymouth - BLs around B 98 7
Plymouth to St. Austell C 63 X
Porthmadog 1954-94 - BL around B 31 6
Porthmadog to Blaenau B 50 2 OOP
Portmadoc 1923-46 - BL around B 13 8
Portsmouths Tramways B 72 3 OOP
Portsmouth to Southampton A 31 2
Portsmouth Trolleybuses C 73 7
Princes Risborough - Branch Lines to D 05 5
Princes Risborough to Banbury C 85 0
R
Railways to Victory C 16 8 OOP
Reading to Basingstoke B 27 8
Reading to Didcot C 79 6
Reading to Guildford A 47 9 OOP
Reading Tramways B 87 1
Reading Trolleybuses C 05 2
Redhill to Ashford A 73 8
Return to Blaenau 1970-82 C 64 8
Roman Roads of Surrey C 61 3
Roman Roads of Sussex C 48 6
Romneyrail C 32 X
Ryde to Ventnor A 19 3
S
Salisbury to Westbury B 39 1
Salisbury to Yeovil B 06 5
Saxmundham to Yarmouth C 69 9
Saxony Narrow Gauge D 28 4
Seaton & Eastbourne T/Ws B 76 6 OOP
Seaton & Sidmouth - Branch Lines to A 95 9
Secret Sussex Resistance B 82 0
SECR Centenary album C 11 7
Selsey - Branch Line to A 04 5 OOP
Sheerness - Branch Lines around B 16 2
Shepherds Bush to Uxbridge T/Ws C 28 1
Shrewsbury - Branch Line to A 86 X
Sierra Leone Narrow Gauge D 28 4
Sittingbourne to Ramsgate A 90 8
Slough to Newbury C 56 7
Solent - Creeks, Crafts & Cargoes D 52 7
Southamptons Tramways B 33 2 OOP

Southampton to Bournemouth A 42 8
Southend-on-Sea Tramways B 28 6
Southern France Narrow Gauge C 47 8
Southwark & Deptford Tramways B 38
Southwold - Branch Line to A 15 0
South Eastern & Chatham Railways C
South London Line B 46 4
South London Tramways 1903-33 D 10
St. Albans to Bedford D 08 X
St. Austell to Penzance C 67 2
St. Pancras to St. Albans C 78 8
Stamford Hill Tramways B 85 5
Steaming through Cornwall B 30 8
Steaming through Kent A 13 4 OOP
Steaming through the Isle of Wight A 5
Steaming through West Hants A 69 X
Stratford-upon-Avon to Cheltenham C
Strood to Paddock Wood B 12 X
Surrey Home Guard C 57 5
Surrey Narrow Gauge C 87 7
Surrey Waterways A 51 7 OOP
Sussex Home Guard C 24 9
Sussex Narrow Gauge C 68 0
Sussex Shipping Sail, Steam & Motor
Swanley to Ashford B 45 6
Swindon to Bristol C 96 6
Swindon to Gloucester D46 2
Swindon to Newport D 30 6
Swiss Narrow Gauge C 94 X
T
Talyllyn - 50 years C 39 7
Taunton to Barnstaple B 60 X
Taunton to Exeter C 82 6
Tavistock to Plymouth B 88 X
Tenterden - Branch Line to A 21 5
Thanet's Tramways B 11 1 OOP
Three Bridges to Brighton A 35 5
Tilbury Loop C 86 9
Tiverton - Branch Lines around C 62 1
Tivetshall to Beccles D 41 1
Tonbridge to Hastings A 44 4
Torrington - Branch Lines to B 37 5
Tunbridge Wells - Branch Lines to A 32
Twickenham & Kingston Trys C 35 4
Two-Foot Gauge Survivors C 21 4 OO
U
Upwell - Branch Line to B 64 2
V
Victoria & Lambeth Tramways B 49 9
Victoria to Bromley South A 98 3
Victoria to East Croydon A 40 1
Vivarais C 31 1
W
Walthamstow & Leyton Tramways B
Waltham Cross & Edmonton Trys C 0
Wandsworth & Battersea Tramways B
Wantage - Branch Line to D 25 X
Wareham to Swanage - 50 yrs D 09 8
War on the Line A 10 X
War on the Line VIDEO + 88 0
Waterloo to Windsor A 54 1
Waterloo to Woking A 38 X
Watford to Leighton Buzzard D 45 4
Wenford Bridge to Fowey C 09 5
Westbury to Bath B 55 3
Westbury to Taunton C 76 1
West Cornwall Mineral Railways D 48
West Croydon to Epsom B 08 1
West London - Branch Lines of C 50 8
West London Line B 84 7
West Sussex Waterways A 24 X
West Wiltshire - Branch Lines of D 12 8
Weymouth - Branch Lines around A 65
Willesden Junction to Richmond B 71 5
Wimbledon to Beckenham C 58 3
Wimbledon to Epsom B 62 6
Wimborne - Branch Lines around A 97
Wisbech - Branch Lines around C 01 X
Wisbech 1800-1901 C 93 1
Woking to Alton A 59 2
Woking to Portsmouth A 25 8
Woking to Southampton A 55 X
Woolwich & Dartford Trolleys B 66 9
Worcester to Hereford D 38 1
Worthing to Chichester A 06 1 OOP
Y
Yeovil - 50 yrs change C 38 9
Yeovil to Dorchester A 76 2
Yeovil to Exeter A 91 6